AMERICAN URBAN
ARCHITECTURE

American Urban Architecture

CATALYSTS IN THE DESIGN OF CITIES

WAYNE ATTOE AND DONN LOGAN

UNIVERSITY OF CALIFORNIA PRESS
Berkeley / Los Angeles / London

University of California Press
Berkeley and Los Angeles, California
University of California Press, Ltd.
London, England
© 1989 by
The Regents of the University of California
Printed in the United States of America
1 2 3 4 5 6 7 8 9

Library of Congress Cataloging-in-Publication Data

Attoe, Wayne.
   American urban architecture : catalysts in the design of cities /
Wayne Attoe and Donn Logan.
     p. cm.
   Includes index.
   ISBN 0-520-06152-7 (alk. paper)
   1. City planning—United States.   2. Architecture—United States.
I. Logan, Donn. II. Title.
NA9105.A87 1989
711′.4′0973—dc19   88-14395

CONTENTS

ACKNOWLEDGMENTS

A number of people have helped us by providing information about developments in several cities: Stephen F. Dragos for Milwaukee and Phoenix; Larry Dully, Becky Spurger, and Chris Kopca in Portland; James Visser in Kalamazoo; Arthur Cotton Moore, Patricia Moore, and George Hartman in Georgetown; and Gerald M. Trimble in San Diego. Jerry Keyser shared observations about events in several cities.

Jean Beckley, Richard Close, Steve Halmo, Susan Hoover, Joe Lengling, Roger Schluntz, John Wellhoefer, and Mary Ellen Young helped to find or prepare special illustrations.

Robert M. Beckley, Sinclair Black, Barry Elbasani, Frank Fuller, Carol Shen Glass, and Marcy Wong read and critiqued early versions of the manuscript. Peter Frith and Robert Mugerauer gave us detailed, useful late readings.

Al Costa, Logan Cravens, Scott Lentz, and Clarence Mamuyac helped in preparing drawings.

Richard Bender brought us together, and Hal Box and the School of Architecture at the University of Texas at Austin supported particular aspects of our work. Stephanie Fay, our editor, brought great care and close attention to all aspects of the transformation from manuscript to book form.

We are grateful to them all.

CREDITS FOR ILLUSTRATIONS

PREFACE

In pre-twentieth-century Europe, cities often reflected common ideas about the design of urban buildings. Typically the form of cities was cohesive, and public spaces were clearly defined because each building played a part in an ensemble. The individual structures on Kramgasse in Berne, Switzerland, were conceived in sympathy with their neighbors and in consideration of their role in defining an outdoor public room. The issue here is not whether these design gestures were spontaneous and purposeful or were required by public policy; rather, it is the common agreement that each building played an important part in continuously generating and regenerating urban places.

A second example underscores the point in a less obvious way. The buildings that line Gråbrødretorv (Gray Brothers Square) in Copenhagen are varied in size, color, and form. Yet they succeed as an urban ensemble because of their ubiquitous small-scale similarities. The major common feature is the pattern of small windows with frames painted white that recurs on every building. Moreover, each has a gabled roof either parallel or perpendicular to the facade; each has a tall distinctive ground floor representing the public or commercial edge of the square; each is painted a distinctive vivid color. Together the buildings create a common frontage. (One can imagine the moral or even legal dilemma of a designer who might have tried to go against this persuasive grain.) The result is a happy blend of individuality and urban responsibility.

In the twentieth century, urban form has derived more often from theory than from such a consensus. Contemporary European urban design theorists have tried to create a new consensus based on different attitudes toward urban form, attitudes often characterized by the terms *functionalist, townscape, structuralist,* and *neo-rationalist* (or *rationalist*). Our concern here is not the application of these attitudes in Europe but rather our belief that European urban design theory in the twentieth century has not provided a sound basis for American urban design. An appropriate urbanism for America must grow out of the inherent characteristics and conditions of American cities, not out of theories derived from an alien experience.

What is distinctively American? Street scenes from Milwaukee, Wisconsin, and Austin, Texas, have a recognizably American character, a

1. Kramgasse, Berne.

2. Gråbrødretorv (Gray Brothers Square), Copenhagen. Photograph by Marcy Wong.

spirit and identity all their own. The broad, straight streets, the robust commercialism, the absence of pre-industrial-age buildings, and the tendency to build as high as possible are aspects of an American urban identity as obvious in these old photographs as they would be in many contemporary views.

Theorists have given little attention to the peculiarities of American cities. Although Jane Jacobs has provided vivid descriptions of American urban districts and the harm done to them by modernist planning,[1] and even though Jonathan Barnett has argued persuasively for zoning and design controls based on the American market system,[2] most American writers have been content either to refer to classical, baroque, functionalist, or vernacular European precedents for notions about building and rebuilding American cities or to espouse the most recent European ideals.[3] Much recent urban development in the United States has been based on a pragmatic picking and choosing among European theories and precedents, with a few homegrown techniques thrown in. But the European theories are unconvincing in American contexts. Instead of the appliqué of imported ideas and homegrown methods, we need an urban design theory that is appropriate to American circumstances and allows architects, urban designers, and planners to develop a consensus about our own urban values.

This book presents such a theory, which we call catalytic architecture. It describes the positive impact an individual urban building or project can have on subsequent projects and, ultimately, the form of a city. It encourages designers, planners, and policymakers to consider the chain-reactive potential of individual developments on civic growth and urban regeneration. It advocates design control as part of a catalytic strategy for urban design.

Those who describe the rebuilding of cities typically employ the metaphors of renewal and revitalization, suggesting with the first a surgical procedure comparable to an organ transplant or a prosthetic implant and with the second the reintroduction of life. Although both metaphors are

3. Milwaukee, Wisconsin, in the late nineteenth century.

4. Austin, Texas, in the early twentieth century.

useful (we use them ourselves) to describe the final results of rebuild-ing—Rochester, New York, for example, was renewed when its dysfunc-tional "heart" was replaced—the process of renewal itself is too radical because it means tearing out too much and replacing it with alien ele-ments, and the process of revitalization is not powerful enough to struc-ture an ongoing regeneration. Catalysis, in contrast, is both an appealing metaphor and an appropriate process for rebuilding, one that is sensitive to its context and also powerful enough to restructure it. The chemical analogy of catalysis accurately describes our approach to urban redevel-opment in the following chapters. We postulate that the strategic intro-duction of new elements can revitalize exisiting ingredients of the urban center without necessarily changing them radically. And even as the cata-lyst stimulates such new life, it also affects the form, character, and quality of urban elements that are subsequently introduced. In short, a controlled catalytic chain reaction takes place.

In the United States urban catalysis is partially established in practice, but not in theory. Most of the revitalization projects undertaken in the past thirty years claim not only to reintroduce vitality through new de-velopment but also to affect surrounding areas. Although development schemes are often described as catalysts capable of changing a city's chemistry, they may in fact do nothing at all, or they may just raise land values, forcing out worthwhile uses of land and buildings that cannot sus-tain the new economics. The term *catalyst* is frequently misused in de-scriptions of the changes incidental to gross investment and new construction in cities, for virtually any improvement will have some effects in adjacent areas, but these effects are haphazard and often harmful. *An architectural catalyst does not simply set off reactions but guides and conditions them too.* In formulating a theory of catalytic urban architecture, we are particularly interested in the way the form of a building or complex influences subsequent constructions. We are interested in the way catalytic architectural forms can shape other forms, as they did in Berne and Copenhagen.

As an example of an urban catalyst, consider Ghirardelli Square in San Francisco. In the early 1960s an obsolete chocolate factory in a nonretail area was converted into a specialty shopping complex. The design had immense power as an urban place because of the richness and strength of the existing buildings and the talent of both the architects, Wurster Bernardi and Emmons, and the landscape architect, Lawrence Halprin, in weaving a pattern of charming plazas, courtyards, and passages between buildings. The economic success of Ghirardelli Square recommended a parallel treatment for the Cannery, a similar specialty center located two blocks away, designed by Joseph Esherick and Associates.

The economic reaction is only part of catalysis, however. Ghirardelli Square also influenced the *form and character* of the Cannery: because the first project was well designed, so was the second. Once the Cannery was in place, as a natural consequence of market forces, buildings along Beach Street between the two nodes were refitted and re-leased. Again, these two seminal efforts affected the form, style, and detail of the new and renovated buildings around them. They truly were architectural, as well as social and economic, catalysts. In urban design terms, Ghirardelli Square made possible a project like the Cannery. The completion of the Cannery strengthened the potential for additional change; it shaped a critical mass. A myriad of changes all around followed, chiefly to the east toward Fisherman's Wharf. Moreover, the two complexes had a wider influence, ushering in the genre of specialty shopping centers in re-used structures and giving momentum and status to the adaptive reuse movement.

Unfortunately, however, the positive influence of architectural catalysis seems to wane as distance from the catalyst increases. A successful pair of catalysts like Ghirardelli Square and the Cannery produce many independent responses in a flurry of bandwagonism; but further from the source, it is less likely that positive, qualitative architectural and urban design influence will hold. If planners and policymakers acknowledged the process of urban catalysis, they could counteract the diminishing influence of individual design actions and thus shape and direct the design of remote as well as nearby development.

The chapters that follow seek to accomplish the following: (1) to demonstrate that although various urban design theories based on the forms and institutions of European cities are useful, they are insufficient to the design needs of American cities; (2) to outline a theory of urban catalysis, based on American urban forms and institutions, that can serve in planning the regeneration of our cities and, using case studies, to demon-

5. *Ghirardelli Square, San Francisco, 1962. Wurster Bernardi and Emmons, architects; Lawrence Halprin, landscape architect.*

strate the usefulness of the catalytic interpretation to urban design practice; (3) to encourage pragmatic Americans to nurture idealism in the context of pragmatic practice (No one ideal is best for all developments in all cities, but aspirations toward an ideal based on American urbanism and the specifics of place will distinguish exceptional from ordinary schemes); (4) to promote the notion that molding the town, the urban place, and the neighborhood is at least as important as designing individual buildings; and (5) to demonstrate the power of individual buildings

6. *The Cannery, San Francisco, 1966. Joseph Esherick and Associates, architects.*

and complexes to affect the form of subsequent design and construction. Others have written and will continue to write about the social, political, and economic impact of one development on another. Our concern is that of architects, so we will speak of the architectural aspects of urban catalysis and will focus on the building blocks, the structures that stimulate and sustain urban chemistry. And although we emphasize catalyzing the sound redevelopment of central cities, it could well be that the catalytic concept has relevance in other contexts as well.

Our motivation in this effort is twofold. First, American urban design tends to focus on how to do rather than on what to do; thus the tools and methods of urban redevelopment are used without a guiding vision. As a result, urban design in America seldom achieves greatness. Second, the guiding visions of European theorists seldom flourish on American soil. We hope to suggest a vision for the urban design process that subsumes the often good and useful but individually inadequate European visions for urban design. In a sense we respond to a plea from Jonathan Barnett, who also recognizes that particular, prescribed patterns traditionally fail. What we need now is not more urban design styles but rather "new ways of integrating city design with the process of economic and social change."[4] We believe that the concept of catalytic urban architecture gives us what we need.

Wayne Attoe, Austin
Donn Logan, Berkeley
Autumn 1988

1

URBAN DESIGN THEORY, EUROPEAN STYLE

From our position as Americans, geographically distant from the theoretical discussions of Europe and faced with needs and circumstances somewhat different from those of European theorists and urban designers, we can distinguish four stances in European theories of urban design in the twentieth century: functionalist, humanist, systemic, and formalist. Instead of attempting to articulate each one and to sort out the disagreements among its various proponents, we find it more useful here to discuss each generically.

These four stances in European urban design are not in themselves precise and internally consistent theories but inclinations, predispositions, or directions. By conceiving of them in this way, we can accommodate the ideas and hopes of a range of individuals in several countries over a number of decades—their values, visions, and means for tackling urban problems. In trying to understand these stances in urban design theory, we asked the following questions:

1. How do the proponents of each stance envision cities?
2. What is the evidence that a particular stance influenced design and planning decisions?
3. What factors are instrumental in achieving environmental design quality?
4. Which decision-making methods are associated with this stance?
5. What is its attitude toward the past?
6. What assumptions do proponents make about the nature and purpose of the urban center?
7. What are typical criticisms of this orientation in urban design?

Our particular concern is the implications for urban regeneration and rejuvenation associated with each stance.

THE FUNCTIONALIST STANCE

Of the four orientations we examine here, functionalism, with the longest history, has been the most comprehensively outlined. Its origins are in the Bauhaus and the work of Le Corbusier; its credo is the Athens

Charter of the Congrès Internationaux d'Architecture Moderne (CIAM),* issued in 1933. Workability and competence are its goals. It is the equivalent in urban planning of the modern movement in architecture. This is not to say that the functionalist view is consistent. It originated in the 1920s and dominated design theory into the 1950s, evolving in response to criticism and changing conditions. In part because of such periodic corrections, we prefer the terms *stance* or *orientation* to the more specific term *theory*. A theory of urban design needs to describe the nature of urban settings, the goals for urban form and use, and a method for realizing the goals that is consistent with the nature of the settings. A stance is similar but less precise. It points to a constellation of individuals with similar values, among whom there can nonetheless be considerable differences of opinion and emphasis.

Functionalism envisions the city as a collection of uses to be accommodated: residence, work, leisure, and the traffic systems that serve them. In early functionalist thought the city was characterized as a machine, in later thought, as a complex organism and as a network or constellation of community centers linked to and directed by a central core.[1] A functionalist city is equitable; it does not favor or neglect social groups. Everyone benefits from adequate sunlight, fresh air, and access to open space.

Functionalist theory treats residence, work, and leisure as discrete elements. Activities should not mix; hence zoning is a key element of the functionalist city, for in a zoned environment, activities can proceed with little or no interference from other activities. In functionalist urban planning, organizing functional relations in a two-dimensional plan usually takes precedence over organizing other relations. The graphics associated with each of the four orientations are telling: functionalist schemes rely heavily on plan drawings, whereas humanist, systemic, and formalist schemes are typified, respectively, by intimate views, diagrams, and bird's-eye perspectives.

Though functionalist theory calls for the separation of activities, in one locale, the heart or core of the city, these must be commingled. The idealized purpose of the urban center is "to enable people to meet one another to exchange ideas." Therefore that center "must be attractive to all types of people in the region it serves"—a place of rendezvous, spontaneity, organized activity, refuge. In sum, the urban center should engender "civic consciousness."[2] It is more than a machine for making money and more than a crossroads for traffic and goods: "The Core includes other elements, often of an imponderable nature."[3] Necessary to the success of the urban center is the absence of vehicular traffic, for the urban center is the domain of pedestrians.

Though not a feature of its dogma, orthogonal planning characterizes most functionalist urban design. Schemes tend to mix formal and asymmetrical elements in a visual treatment that seems all of a piece because of the underlying rectilinear format. This admixture seems to satisfy a fur-

*CIAM, founded in 1928, formalized and proselytized the precepts of modern architecture.

7. *In the ideogram summarizing the functionalist stance, orthogonal planning is set within the organic framework of the medieval city. The grain of the functionalist plan is regular and includes much open space. Based on a plan for Coventry, England, published in* Architect and Building News, *21 March 1941.*

ther functionalist goal—that contemporary towns exhibit contemporary (constructivist, cubist) means of expression.[4]

The quality of functionalist design depends on how competently it accommodates needs and activities and on how well it uses light, space, and greenery, the ingredients of an urban plan that enhance daily experience. Open space is highly valued—not vast spaces but controlled, demarcated spaces adjacent to functional areas. This value may be seen as a reaction to crowded conditions in medieval towns and nineteenth-century industrial cities.

Functionalist theory calls for research, a thorough analysis of needs and circumstances, and a deliberative decision-making process by trained professionals. They must coordinate natural, sociological, economic, and other factors specific to the cultural context and stage of development. Planning anticipates rather than responds: "Intelligent forecasts will have sketched its future, described its character, foreseen the extent of its expansions, and limited their excesses in advance."[5]

Whereas functionalist thinking is associated with Le Corbusier and CIAM, Constantine Doxiadis's later ekistic theory may be seen as a "correction" and elaboration of that tradition. Ekistic principles include (1) being realistic; (2) thinking at long range and with broad scope; (3) identifying, evaluating, and classifying problems to be addressed; (4) establishing policies to guide decisions; (5) devising plans that follow from those policies; (6) evaluating constantly; and (7) reappraising periodically.[6]

According to the functionalist view, historically significant buildings should be preserved for their educational value, but the layout of historic districts should not be the basis for planning contemporary towns. Urban developments that occurred by chance or grew from particular historical imperatives are notorious for their inhumane living conditions. Medieval precincts of cities and industrial slums are evidence of inadequate methods for urban development.

Critics of functionalism argue that it deals with urban design only impersonally, at a large scale: "A land-use master plan for a big city is largely a matter of proposed placement, often in relation to transportation, of many series of decontaminated sortings."[7] The human scale is often neglected. Then, too, the general categories that functionalism considers, like residence and traffic, fail to acknowledge subtleties. In fact these variables may well be the wrong ones to begin with in urban design, for they do not take into account "the personality of the inhabitants" and are "too often inhuman."[8] The functionalist vision is "negative" because "it con-

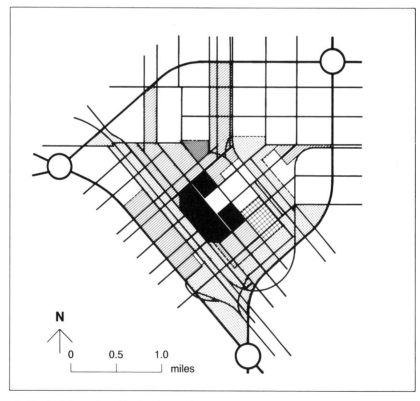

8. *Typical functionalist land use plan. Derived from a Victor Gruen scheme for Fresno, California.*

ceives of buildings merely as scaffolding for functional variations, abstract containers that embody whatever functions successively fill them."[9] Separation and zoning may ameliorate nuisance and the interference of functional parts, but such a division of activities also works against richness. The hustle and bustle of downtown, or of a neighborhood center, are impossible when uses are sorted out and treated in standardized ways: "A hierarchy of human associations should replace the functional hierarchy of the *Charte d'Athènes.*"[10]

Functionalist designers are accused of responding to superficial and ephemeral wants, fashions, and pressures rather than to long-standing cultural traditions. For some critics this concern with the transitory is a manifestation of bourgeois, capitalist culture: "The vulgarity of late capitalist architecture is as much caused by the random profusion of building types as by the endless invention of building materials and construction systems; [it is] not an outcome of rationalisation but of maximisation of profits."[11]

Finally, the singlemindedness of the functionalist stance threatens to overwhelm regional and cultural differences. Functional analysis describes rather than explains the city: "It does not posit any element of continuity between the *genre de vie* and the urban structure."[12] "We are willing to accept functional classification as a practical and contingent criterion, the equivalent of a number of other criteria—for example, social make-up, constructional system, development of the area, and so on— since such classifications have a certain utility; nonetheless it is clear that they are more useful for telling us about the point of view adopted for classification than about an element itself."[13]

THE HUMANIST STANCE

The humanist position is not as clearly and comprehensively formulated as the functionalist. Rather, it is a collection of intentions, techniques, and design ideas offered by a diverse group of proponents. It emerged in the 1950s and 1960s not as a new theory but as a reaction to the unsatisfactory results of functionalist thinking and design. Among those representing humanist attitudes were the British townscape school, disaffected CIAM members who took the name Team 10, and certain Dutch architects.*

Although both functionalist and humanist approaches are responsive to needs, the former begins at the macro scale, with zoning for industry, housing, and so forth and necessary transport connections, whereas the latter begins by examining the impact of small-scale elements on day-to-day experiences:

---

*Kenneth Browne, Gordon Cullen, and Thomas Sharp are most closely associated with townscape values, the concern for richness and responsiveness in small-scale urban environments. Team 10 included Alison Smithson, Peter Smithson, Aldo van Eyck, Georges Candillis, and Jacob Bakema. The Dutch architects with humanist/structuralist inclinations include Herman Hertzberger and Aldo van Eyck.

9. An ideogram for humanist urban design recalls the drawings of Gordon Cullen and Kenneth Browne. Humanist qualities are suggested in the visual variety, attention to small scale, depiction of people engaged in activities, and annotations through which the designer "scripts" the place. From a drawing by Kenneth Browne, published in West End *(London: Architectural Press, 1971).*

Make a welcome of each door
a countenance of each window.
Make of each a place; a bunch of places of each house and each city
(a house is a tiny city, a city a huge house).[14]

Functionalist planning imposes a structure upon the city, whereas humanist planning seeks to realize and enhance preexisting and underlying social structures. Land-use diagrams are typical illustrative techniques for functionalist schemes; a humanist design is more likely to be described with a set of sequential drawings depicting a user's perception of the place and conveying a variegated visual character or with a diagram of behavioral patterns.

For those whose first concern is the human experience of the city and its social life, the good city is best understood as a collection of enclaves not unlike villages. These are shaped by and reflect the individuals and groups who inhabit them. Humanist designers expect the inhabitants of a city to "appropriate" the environment and make it their own; they believe that the city should not be a fait accompli but that people should specify and help to create what they want. Self-help and reliance on neighbors are better than dependency on a centralized government: "The more somebody is personally able to influence his surroundings, the more involved and attentive he becomes, and also the more likely he will be to give them his love and care. What we offer cannot be neutral; it must be the raw material, as it were, containing the 'intentions' out of which everyone can make his own choice in a particular situation, extracting from it precisely the intention which 'resonates' with his intentions."[15] In other cases where the design task is more complicated, an advocate intervenes on behalf of users to improve what producers offer.

Decisions are based on users' needs and circumstances rather than on concepts: "The best way to plan for downtown is to see how people use it today; to look for its strengths and to exploit and reinforce them. There is no logic that can be superimposed on the city; people make it, and it is to them, not buildings, that we must fit our plans."[16] Decision making tends to be incremental rather than set by a master plan. Insofar as centralized planning is needed, its goal should be to "catalyze" and "nourish" rather than to direct: "The science of city planning and the art of city design, in real life for real cities, must become the science and art of catalyzing and nourishing . . . close-grained working relationships."[17]

Whereas on the small scale inhabitants mold the city in a multitude of ways as they pursue myriad personal visions, at the larger scale there are meaningful "monuments" that represent an enduring shared heritage, neither transient nor personal. Acknowledging this difference, Dutch humanist architects distinguish between special buildings of enduring character and everyday architecture that serves the immediate needs and desires of the populace. For them the city thus both reflects the evolving requirements of its inhabitants and testifies to timeless cultural values and patterns. Present and past intertwine. For Aldo van Eyck, "the time has come to bring together the old into the new; to rediscover the archaic principles of human nature."[18]

The humanist urban designer pays attention to small-scale elements and informal ordering systems, avoiding large-scale, superimposed geometries. Design in human scale achieves familiarity and the sense that things have been made by and for people. Van Eyck affirms the importance of fitting architecture to the people who inhabit it; the mission of architecture, in other words, is to assist in man's homecoming.[19]

Humanist designers, moreover, advocate a mixed use of the urban environment. Functional zoning and functional distinctions are not the norm; instead, activities and elements overlap and are interwoven so the "drama is released."[20] For example, whereas functionalist streets are principally for automobiles, humanist streets are domesticated and become "livable" places "for people."[21] "In the suburbs and slums the vital relation-ship between the house and the street survives, children run about, . . . people stop and talk, dismantled vehicles are parked, . . . you know the milkman, you are outside your house in your street. . . . Streets [should] be places and not corridors or balconies. Thoroughfares where there are shops, post boxes, telephone kiosks."[22] When traffic hazards, noise, and pollution are controlled on these streets, the pavements become a stage for the theater of neighborhood life.[23] Urban character comes from a rich mix, what Jane Jacobs calls "organized complexity."

Humanists believe that the future city need not differ much from the present one insofar as the present one is satisfactory. Any changes that are needed will be patterned more often on elements of existing neigh-borhoods and districts than on new concepts. In effect, tradition is a sourcebook of these elements that were thrown out or ignored by func-tionalist design, which sought to invent a new and different future. Hu-manist urban design finds lessons in the past, among them specific bor-rowable features that make places visually more appealing and more congenial: kiosks, bollards, granite pavers, benches, and so forth. Human-ist designers also borrow from vernacular traditions such qualities and patterns as market squares, passages, and clustered housing. Because they suspect direct imitation and worry about pastiche and phoniness, human-ist urban designers translate borrowed ideas from the past into modern terms whenever possible. Humanists like Aldo van Eyck complain that "modern architects have been harping continually on what is different in our time to such an extent that even they have lost touch with what is not different, with what is always essentially the same."[24]

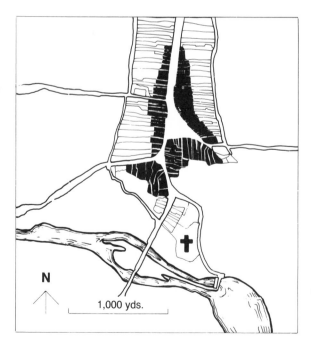

10. A traditional village mixes uses at a human scale and thus is a model for humanist design. Based on a plan in Maurice Beresford, New Towns of the Middle Ages *(London: Lutterworth, 1967).*

Whereas a functionalist urban designer might conceive of the urban center as a place for the impersonal exchange of goods and information and thus design it to be efficient for this process, the humanist designer sees the center as enhancing the human experience of these activities. Intimacy and richness of experience must go hand in hand with efficiency. The urban center is not so much a tool of commerce as a richly variegated composite of experiences. Designers must consider "what makes a city center magnetic, what can inject the gaiety, the wonder, the cheerful hurly-burly that make people want to come into the city and to linger there. For magnetism is the crux of the problem. All downtown's values are its by-products. To create in it an atmosphere of urbanity and exuberance is not a frivolous aim." [25]

Critics say that humanists do not consider the large-scale issues and overall needs of the city. Although *houses* may be designed at the grass roots, *housing* is a system that needs a comprehensive perspective and approach. The incremental planning that characterizes the humanist method can create problems in the workings of the larger urban system. And the design-by-committee approach inherent in humanist theory slows down improvement and makes conflict inevitable. The future of cities is too complex a task for the naive and the untrained.

The efforts of the humanist designer to achieve small-scale familiarity often result in pastiche. In appealing to the senses, such a design often fails the mind. It focuses on perceived surfaces and neglects and devalues deeper concepts.[26] In short, it can be little more than scenographic.

THE SYSTEMIC STANCE

The systemic approach emphasizes large-scale elements of urban design and seeks an overall order for the urban place. Its Team 10 proponents asserted "comprehensibility" as an overriding value.[27] Systemic theory accepts urbanization and increasing societal complexity as inevitable. The key to successful urban design in a complex world is organizing the underlying systems, not individual buildings.

Although systemic theory gives priority to large-scale urban ordering, exactly what is ordered can vary. For some urban design theorists, achieving diagrammatic clarity in transportation systems is the principal task: "Today our most obvious failure is the lack of comprehensibility and identity in big cities, and the answer is surely in a clear, large scale road system—the 'Urban Motorway' lifted from an ameliorative function to a unifying function." [28] Flow and movement are the source of architecture; expressways order the city. For other designers, particularly certain Dutch architects, urban structure results from a physical armature ("support") to which "detachable units" are added: "An area can be differentiated over which the individual has control and another over which the community collectively decides." [29] Recognizing that both transportation and shelter must be accommodated, some systemic urban design solutions integrate the two systems. The city, for them, is an interlocked system of movement corridors and structural armatures supporting housing and other uses.

From a practical point of view, overall urban ordering is necessary because of the demands of vehicular traffic, the dependency of modern life on communications, and the need for the rapid, continuous production of building elements. Efficiency in communications is achieved, in part, by separating modes of transportation; the possibility of conflict is reduced when, for example, high-speed and low-speed movement are separated and when pedestrians are removed from vehicular systems. But the rapid growth of cities and the deterioration of aging buildings also necessitate efficiency. The assembly-line production of building elements seems necessary to satisfy burgeoning demands for both new and replacement shelter. As a consequence, elements of such urban systems favor an industrial aesthetic. Systems designers advise developing "an aesthetic appropriate to mechanized building techniques and scales of operation" because such a correlation of form and manufacture is rational. Further, they find much mass housing to be culturally obsolescent and prefer "a genuinely twentieth-century technological image of the dwelling—comfortable, safe and not feudal." [30]

One innovation of systemic thinking is the notion that areas do not have to be cleared for rejuvenation to take place. Functionalist theory presupposes a clean slate, but systemic theory proposes that linear systems (of movement, of new construction) be woven into and around existing structures. Instead of conceiving of the urban fabric as a collection of building masses, systemic design treats it as a dynamic web of connections. Systems are conceived as able to grow and change incidentally without compromising the underlying order. Change of this sort is assumed to be a feature of modern life. The contrast between simple, abstract, orderly patterns and complex existing patterns is marked, as schemes by Yona Friedman and Kenzo Tange demonstrate—one hovering above a traditional city, the other harbored adjacent to it.

11. The ideogram for the systemic orientation emphasizes the dimensionless underlying order, which remains despite additions and subtractions. Based on a design for Caen-Herouville by Shadrach Woods, published in Urbanism Is Everybody's Business *(Stuttgart: Karl Krämer, 1968).*

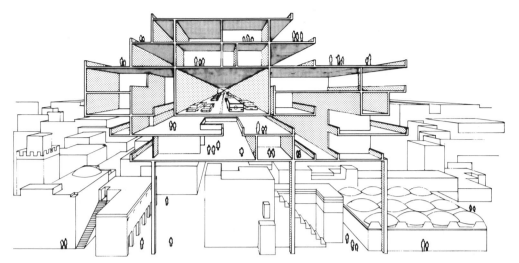

12. *A new urban structure imposed upon an older fabric. Based on a drawing by Yona Friedman in* L'Architecture Mobile *(Tournai, Belgium: Casterman, 1970.*

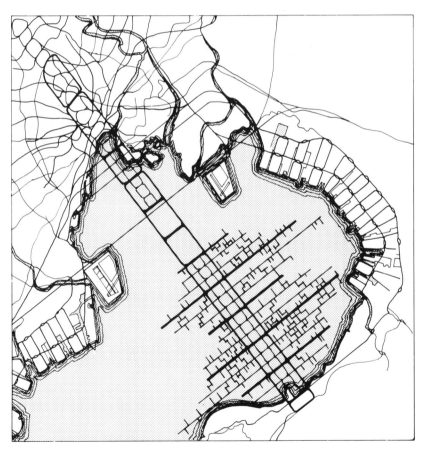

13. *Kenzo Tange's Tokyo Bay Project. After a drawing published in* Japan Architect *(April 1961). Tange proposed a highly structured extension of Tokyo into Tokyo Bay.*

Whereas we use the term *systemic* to refer to this stance in urban design theory, others sometimes use the term *structuralist.* This difference in terminology is a potential source of confusion when, for example, Kenzo Tange uses the term *structuring* in discussing the systems concept. He calls for "networks of communication" imitating a living body and the ability of the structure to grow and change.[31] Identifying this stance in urban design theory as *structuralist* may cause confusion because Claude Lévi-Strauss and others use the term to refer to anthropological concepts. Although Tange's structure and the anthropologists' and others' structuralism have some common concerns, they are fundamentally different ideas. Systemic structure *imposes* an order upon the world; structuralist structure *finds* inherent order, finds similarities between social patterns in African villages and industrial slums, for example.

Anthropological structuralism, although it can inform systemic design and planning, falters as a guide. Lévi-Strauss himself pointed out that to search for underlying order is not the same as imposing order on phenomena.[32] In effect, structuralist anthropologists have the luxury of analyzing what exists and stopping, whereas systems-oriented urban designers must analyze and then build. For example, Alison and Peter Smithson's studies of association and identity in neighborhoods led to the development of "systems of linked building complexes, which were intended to correspond more closely to the network of social relationships, as they now exist [in cities], than the existing patterns of finite spaces and self-contained buildings."[33] The anthropological concept of structure is relevant to our discussion. But instead of associating it with one theoretical orientation, like systemic theory, we find aspects of it in several of the approaches to urban design. Systemic, humanist, and even formalist theories in one way or another each reflect certain structuralist premises and concerns.

In architecture, structuralism in the anthropological sense is most often associated with Dutch architects like Herman Hertzberger and Aldo van Eyck and with a particular concern to make places that are meaningful. In that context more often than not it refers to building design rather than urban design. When Dutch structuralists design at the larger urban scale, their structuralism resembles Tange's structuring (what we call systemic thinking) and is related less to human behavior, than to the goal of having structures that can be modified to suit changing circumstances. Team 10 architects whom we identify with the humanist stance sometimes evidence structuralist values.

Because town building must respond to the scale of movement systems,[34] and systemic design tends to be abstract, designs for specific details are often absent. It is not that the human scale is of no concern but that design at the small scale apparently is left to others or to another stage of the design process. The unit of order, instead of being buildings as it has been traditionally, is now the connective system.

The extensive character of systemic urban design means that decision making must be centralized and guided by trained planners and architects. Typically they begin by seeking (or imposing) an underlying structure of movement. Other decisions follow. The design of smaller parts may be undertaken by others, even by groups of citizens and by individuals, for some advocates of the systemic approach assume that such participation at the smaller scale of design "humanizes" the system. Others, however, assume that because the design of the parts linked by the system must be technologically sophisticated, it requires trained designers.

Most proponents of systemic urban design accept obsolescence as a fact of modern industrial civilization. Although they believe that the underlying urban system remains intact, they assume that its elements are added to or replaced in a continuing program of improvement: "To understand and use the possibilities offered by a 'throwaway' technology, [we must] create a new sort of environment with different cycles of change for different functions."[35] Improvements include both the substitution of workable for worn-out parts and the incorporation of new elements to meet the changing needs of inhabitants.

Modern transportation and modern industrial production, in particular, have made large parts of the city of the past obsolete. Because future needs and circumstances will also differ from those of both the past and the present, the very parts that constitute the city must be disposable. Nonetheless, even with the changes necessary to counter obsolescence, the urban framework will remain as the structure, the system within which changes occur.

Because it conceives of the city as a web or network that does not depend upon a center, systemic theory has little to say about the urban core. In the case of multi-nucleated urban settings, the historical center might have a specialized role as a repository and center of culture and the arts. Or it might be the focus of finance. But conceptually it would be only one of several foci of activity.

According to its critics, systemic design ignores the validity and workability of established physical and social fabrics: systemic solutions do not necessarily improve on the past; they uproot existing patterns and introduce alien ones.

Moreover, even though the clarity of systemic approaches improves the legibility of the urban fabric and the efficiency of its operation, smaller-scale, "messy," life-enhancing considerations are left to chance. Many designers favoring systemic approaches acknowledge the importance of small-scale "grain" but do not always specify how the development of an appropriate life-enhancing grain can be assured.

Finally, critics point out that although the vast systems with changeable components must of necessity be produced with modern industrial technologies, the concomitant industrial aesthetic is alien to many people.

THE FORMALIST STANCE

What we call formalist approaches are those that value particular archetypal or universal configurations of urban space and form. For Beaux-Arts planners,* these configurations most often entailed axial organizations and static spaces drawing upon elementary geometries. These reflected a notion of universal order and harmony. More recently, for neo-rationalist designers, for example, who are interested in a less regular "public realm," these configurations have been the streets, squares, and public monuments that structure urban fabrics.

Given the dramatically different socio-economic associations of Beaux-Arts and neo-rationalist practice (the first with hierarchical and upper-middle class values, the second with collective form and populist ideology), it may seem curious to find them linked here as "formalist." Granted, their motives and methods are not similar, but the focus of both is physical form and its associational meanings. And each assumes the existence of timeless design figures from which urban design should be drawn. These are discovered in part through the study of typologies and precedents: "A few building materials and the elaboration of an urban building typology will create a new architectural discipline of simple nobility and monumentality." [36]

In finding sufficiency in earlier forms, the formalist stance lacks the forward-looking idealism of other theories that assume a better way of doing things can be found if we abandon inadequate old methods and seek workable new ones. Instead, formalism argues that satisfactory patterns for accommodating human need and nurturing the spirit exist in our cultural and urban heritage. For example, for neo-rationalists, a particular feature of older cities that has been lost through functionalist land-use zoning is the richness of cities-within-the-city, *quartiers* or districts that integrate all the functions of urban life.

Although it would be easy to characterize the formalist stance as backward-looking idealism, most formalist discourse does not in fact characterize the past as a better time to which we should return but maintains only that traditional solutions contain ideas that work and that these ideas carry with them the ingredient of memory that new architectural forms and new urban spaces inevitably lack. Neo-rationalism does not propose the replication of historical urban fabrics but the use of the past as a filter through which the future is conceived. For Beaux-Arts designers the past was a collection of examples from which to learn, examples that are themselves variations on valued precedents. Thus buildings from the past, forms with cultural significance, lead design insofar as they are good and workable.

Though neo-rationalist and Beaux-Arts formalism originated in formal ordering systems, their products have differed in scale and texture. The neo-rationalist city is a collage of patterned solids and voids. Its parts are imbued with what might be called poetic tension growing from the inherent opposition of solid and void, of figure and ground. Some parts are unabashedly grand and intended as "public realm," whereas other parts are pointedly unassuming private realms. Leon Krier describes the countervailing elements as public "monuments" and "anonymous fabric." The

---

*The principles of these planners evolved from the teachings and designs associated with the Ecole des Beaux-Arts in Paris during the nineteenth century.

14. The ideogram for the formalist stance distinguishes between public realms and the anonymous urban fabric, the former comprising familiar urban forms like the square, avenue, and monument and elemental architectural treatments like the arcade.

parts of which the urban collage is composed refer to historical spaces and forms but are reinterpretations rather than replicas. The city and its buildings do not necessarily seek to satisfy specific needs (as functionalist buildings do) but accommodate changing patterns of use in timeless forms.

Whereas neo-rationalist formalism tends towards a heterogeneous collage, Beaux-Arts urban design favors hierarchy and extensive axial ordering systems; its urban fabric includes many figural buildings, buildings striving not for anonymity but for identity.

According to Anthony Vidler, a rational architecture "is clearly based on reason, classification and a sense of the public in architecture."[37] From our point of view, "reason" means open-minded observation and straightforward methods of production. "Classification" takes the form of seeing and valuing traditional patterns of urban space and building form (typological and morphological studies). "A sense of the public in architecture" means poetry. The approach is conservative, yet there is also room for imagination and change within the tradition. In Beaux-Arts design, too, appropriate precedent is chosen and modified to suit particular necessities. Always there is a dialogue between the universal and the particular.

For neo-rationalists, incremental action is preferable to large-scale, comprehensive action: "With respect to urban intervention today one should operate on a limited part of the city. . . . Such a self-imposed limitation is a more realistic approach from the standpoint of both knowledge and program."[38] In the Beaux-Arts mode, the intervention was more often an extensive restructuring, a correcting of earlier circumstantial and limited visions.

The urban center is the means and the symbol of public life. It makes possible and dignifies collective activities. It is a reflection of long-standing urban traditions, evocative and deeply memorable. Paradoxically, although neo-rationalist theory does not define the urban center, it nonetheless considers that center the essence of urbanism, the place where strands of life are brought together. An urban center in Beaux-Arts terms would be hierarchically the grandest, the noblest, the best embodiment of order, proportion, and harmony. Its value is formal, not experiential or functional. It would symbolize more than it would weave urban life.

Formalist urban design is criticized for being concerned largely with aesthetic matters and only incidentally with real needs: "Successful urban forms often are the product of less than admirable social conditions."[39] The CIAM criticism of City Beautiful design was similar: "Urbanism can no longer submit exclusively to the rules of gratuitous aestheticism. It is functional by its very nature."[40] Jane Jacobs's criticism of formalism reiterates the theme: "There is a quality even meaner than outright ugliness or disorder, and this meaner quality is the dishonest mask of pretended order, achieved by ignoring or suppressing the real order that is struggling to exist and be served. . . . It is futile to plan a city's appearance, or speculate on how to endow it with a pleasing appearance of order, without knowing what sort of innate, functioning order it has."[41]

Critics of formalist thinking argue that neither nostalgia for a timeless past nor utopian visions of the future guarantee good architecture.[42] Nor do they accept with resignation the view that mankind is unchanging.[43] Further, they ask if it is realistic for neo-rationalist architects to advocate a return to a crafts tradition in light of real building economics.[44]

Although much is constant in human life and culture, changes are neither insignificant nor necessarily inconsequential. Vehicular traffic is a fact of modern urban life that cannot be ignored, and traditional urban patterns are incapable of accommodating it. What should be done when the existing urban fabric is inappropriate to new needs or is otherwise unsatisfactory? (It is worth noting that neo-rationalists tend to ignore the automobile and act as if it will disappear, whereas systemic theory comes close to making a fetish of vehicular movement, letting it structure urban form.)

Finally, are medieval and Renaissance urban fabrics in Europe really generic and universally appropriate, even in the vast regions of the world that have developed in the last one hundred to two hundred years? Critics of formalism point out, for example, that "the square is at present an anachronism, having succumbed to the popularity of the supermarket, the telephone, and the television."[45] And although still other distinctive urban patterns might have grown from local conditions in other regions and be available as models, what if there are no such historical elements to constitute a tradition, or what if historical patterns are inadequate to serve contemporary needs? In short, is the structure of European cities or any historical urbanism as universally appropriate as neo-rationalist theory suggests?

THE PROBLEM OF EUROPEAN-BASED THEORIES

We submit that European theory tends to be narrow and argumentative. Each new approach seems to have developed to oppose and replace others, but because all the approaches shift laterally, no single one can encompass the others. We see the alternative approaches in European urban design that we have outlined as complementary and overlapping, but not as sufficient. In the accompanying diagram we characterize European urban design theories as sharing some concerns and values but, more significant, as moving in different directions.

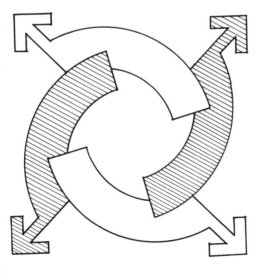

SYSTEMIC

Develop the road and communication systems as the urban infrastructure. (Motorways as a unifying force.) And realize the implication of flow and movement in the architecture itself.—*Forum (Holland) 7*

It is the basic theme of present-day urban design to think of the spatial organization as a network of communication and as a living body with growth and change. This is the process I call "structuring." We need a process of coupling the functional units.—*Kenzo Tange*

The main aim of urbanization is comprehensibility, *i.e.* clarity of organization.—*Alison and Peter Smithson*

HUMANIST

It's getting cold again over here—and always when it does I start thinking about how to warm up architecture, how to make it lodge around us. After all, people buy clothes and shoes the right size and know when the fit feels good. It's time we invented the built thing that fits them—us.—*Aldo van Eyck*

The more somebody is personally able to influence his surroundings, the more involved and attentive he becomes, and also the more likely he will be to give them his love and care.—*Herman Hertzberger*

FORMALIST

We don't have knowledge of everyone's personal images and associations with forms, but we assume that they can be seen as individual interpretations of a collective pattern.—*Herman Hertzberger*

FUNCTIONALIST

Once the city is defined as a functional unit, it should grow harmoniously in each of its parts, having at hand spaces and intercommunications within which the stages of its development may be inscribed with equilibrium. The city will take on the character of an enterprise that has been carefully studied in advance and subjected to the rigor of an overall plan. Intelligent forecasts will have sketched its character, foreseen the extent of its expansions, and limited their excesses in advance.—*Athens Charter, Part 84*

The street. The square. There are almost no other discoveries to be made in architecture.—*Rob Krier*

One is struck by the multiplicity of functions that a building of this type [Palazzo della Ragione in Padua] can contain over time and how these functions are entirely independent of the form. At the same time, it is precisely the form that impresses us; we live it and experience it, and in turn it structures the city.—*Aldo Rossi*

15. Countervailing directions of European theory, with associated testimonies.

Our view, which will emerge in the chapters that follow, is that we need not argue with the values and methods represented by the European heritage of urban design theory. We should not have to abandon the precepts of functionalism to seek the poetry of formalism, or those of humanism to seek urban order, and so forth. The question we ask is not, Which of these European theories should the American designer choose or disregard? but, Which of these intentions should be considered first when the urban designer faces a particular design problem? And then which should be considered next? And we ask, What theory of urban design can translate the European heritage into American terms?

Before we begin to reformulate this diagram according to American contexts, we want to review briefly the impact of European theory on an American city. If our first point is that European theories are unnecessarily argumentative and narrow, our second is that European theory has not fared well in America. Although the cultural link between Europe and America is strong, there are significant differences too. For example, European theory seems often to derive from social objectives, whereas American practice often grows from assumed economic opportunities or imperatives. Because of these differences, an American approach to urban design theory is needed if we are to do good things in American cities.

2

URBAN DESIGN PRACTICE, EURO-AMERICAN STYLE

Just as architectural languages were brought to America by immigrants from Europe, so too recent urban design theory has been a European import. And like architectural styles that came before, European ideas about guiding urban building have been adopted and employed largely without scrutiny. Does this heritage of European urban design theory and practice in fact provide a satisfactory basis for revitalizing and sustaining American towns and cities? The answer is a qualified no. This chapter characterizes the ways in which the four directions in European urban design theory discussed in the preceding chapter have been transposed to American cities and have failed.

First, however, an explanation is needed. Why do the ideas of people like Lewis Mumford, Clarence Stein, Edmund Bacon, Victor Gruen, Jonathan Barnett, Paul Spreiregen, Kevin Lynch, Christopher Alexander, and Frank Lloyd Wright not constitute a distinctive, appropriate, and American urban design theory? In his criticism of planning practice and his praise of particular urban qualities, Mumford has evidenced urban values but has not offered what can be called a theory of urban design. Stein's values and practice were closely related to functionalist thinking in Europe, though with greater attention to small-scale humanist concerns than many functionalist European schemes. But Stein did not formulate a comprehensive theory of urban design related to the development or rejuvenation of urban centers in America. His focus was on new towns with a suburban cast: "The sane policy is first to direct our energy toward building new and complete communities from the ground up: that is to say on open land outside developed urban areas." The "obsolete patterns" of existing cities should be replaced comprehensively, following the model for new towns.[1] In his schemes for Philadelphia, Bacon offers not a unique American vision but a reflection of the systemic and formalist concern for efficient movement and for the aesthetics of urban design.

Victor Gruen's impact on American cities is perhaps greater than that of any other individual, and his model of an urban core circumscribed by trafficways, handy parking lots, and a pedestrian mall is a feature of many urban plans. But Gruen proposes not a theory of urban design so much as a stock solution to the problems of cities choked with cars. The roots of his proposals are European; and although his willingness to admit the importance of the automobile gives his schemes a recognizably American cast, he constructs no theory about the nature of the urban setting or about broad goals and the methods to achieve them. Furthermore, his underlying assumption that the foci of the urban core are shopping and parking is too limited.

Barnett's work, which has spurred and supported urban design in America, is devoted principally to methods of implementing goals rather than to defining them for the urban setting. Hamid Shirvani's book *The Urban Design Process* is more comprehensive.[2] But even though it identifies certain values, design processes, and implementation tools, it offers no theoretical construct to link them. *Urban Design: The Architecture of Towns and Cities,* by Paul Spreiregen, offers historical and recent examples of urban form, techniques, and programs but no theory to guide the process. Kevin Lynch's *Theory of Good City Form* would seem promising, but even he admits that his theory is only "partial."[3] His book considers form but not process, and it strives for a universal theory of urban form, not one keyed to places (for example, American cities). In Lynch's work, like that of the others, we find value but not sufficiency.

Christopher Alexander's "new theory of urban design" seems in sympathy with our view that actions taken in the city need to recognize what already exists and that the process of interaction is what counts. But by his own admission his theory does not acknowledge the economic, ownership, and political realities of American cities. Moreover, it does not draw its lessons from American cities as they are but rather from an academic exercise. The quality on which his theory focuses—wholeness—is good; but like other theorists, he cites mostly non-American towns to exemplify the quality. It is our contention that the foreign settings that have the quality of wholeness probably were not the products of theories but of processes very much like those we describe below.[4]

If any American can be credited with an urban vision distinguishable from European precedents, it is Wright. His Broadacres idea assumes that land is readily available and affordable, that everyone needs personal transportation, and that people prefer suburban settings to living in cities. These assumptions and values are integral to his conception of democracy and contrast sharply with what he calls the monarchical European tendency toward centralization of government, services, and housing: "As centralization was the natural 'monarchy,' . . . men were compelled to centralize and revolve as closely as possible around an exalted common center, for any desirable exploitation of the man-unit. The idea of democracy is contrary. Decentralization—reintegrated—is the reflex: many free units developing strength as they learn to function and grow together in adequate space, mutual freedom a reality."[5] But the focus of our analysis is the possibilities and potential for existing urban centers, not alternatives to urbanization like Broadacre City.

To explore the impact of European urban design theory in America and to see how it falls short, we examine a typical American situation, an industrial city of nineteenth-century origin whose urban center declined economically and deteriorated physically as a result of suburban development and normal aging. Our method, reflected in the following lists, is to identify the problems and their causes and then to see how developments based on European models have fared in the revitalizing of this American city.

Typical Causes of Center City Decline

1. Loss of housing and employment from the city center

2. Exodus of retail activities from the center

3. Increased use of automobiles because of inadequate public transportation

4. Congestion, inconvenience, and reduced environmental quality because of automobile traffic and parking

5. Abandonment of outdated and inadequate buildings and facilities in the older city center in favor of newer facilities elsewhere

6. The association of downtown with environmental deterioration and undesirable social groups—derelicts, the poor, those who are different from most middle-class Americans

7. Cost and difficulty in assembling land for development

8. Deteriorating and costly infrastructure

Typical Motivations for City Center Improvement

1. Damaged civic pride because an economically, physically, and socially weak city center makes a poor impression

2. A persistent image of what a city center should be

3. Declining sales tax revenues

4. Declining property and income tax revenues as businesses and wealthy residents leave the center city

5. The loss of jobs to competing suburban employment centers

6. Loss of residents

7. Deterioration of buildings, infrastructure, and environmental quality

8. Increasing crime

With these problems to solve and these motivations for solving them, Americans in the last three or four decades have initiated projects to reverse the decline of city centers. Because there was nothing like a corpus of American urban design theory on which to draw, urban reclamation efforts in America have relied either on expediency (what can be done easily and cheaply that will solve problems for the time being) or on planning ideals drawn from European theories. Some of the American applications of European ideas are striking and well known. For example, New York's Stuyvesant Town closely resembles Le Corbusier's functionalist schemes for Paris and elsewhere. Pruitt-Igoe in St. Louis and Robert Taylor "homes" in Chicago similarly grew from Corbusian or post-Bauhaus images and reasoning. Like other American versions of European ideals, these are watered down or, perhaps, to be fairer, beaten back with laments about cost and government intervention and waste of money. Most often American versions of European ideas fail for lack of capital or conviction and inadequate analysis of context and need.

As a case study we examine Milwaukee, Wisconsin, and its efforts to build foreign ideals in an American city. Established in the late eighteenth century, Milwaukee a century later was a thriving export center for grain and an industrial center that for a time outshone and then rivaled Chicago. As in many American cities of the period, immigrants formed a substantial part of the population, so it is not surprising that ideals for the city's development often had a foreign cast. One early instance is particularly noteworthy. A development called Garden Homes was probably the earliest example of publicly supported housing in the United States. The city and county of Milwaukee invested in the Garden Homes cooperative development, which drew inspiration from British model towns like Port Sunlight, Letchworth, Bourneville, and Hampstead Garden Suburb (all of which were commemorated as street names in the Garden Homes development). The concept of a cooperative ownership program seems to have been drawn from Germany. The dream of affordable owner-occupied housing for the working class was short-lived, however. Only 105 housing units were built between 1923 and 1927, when the project was liquidated. This European ideal was only the first to fail in Milwaukee's increasingly Americanized soil.[6]

It is to more recent efforts at urban development and revitalization that we address ourselves, however, in particular, the reaction to suburbanization. Like many other cities, Milwaukee suffered from the exodus to the suburbs following World War II. Remote shopping centers competed with and then outdistanced the downtown retail center. The federal bulldozer and riots in the 1960s sped the decline. By the early 1970s the city's downtown was fourteenth in sales among the region's fourteen shopping centers. Milwaukee has a relatively stable population of 750,000 in a growing metropolitan region of roughly 1,500,000.

In considering Milwaukee's efforts to reconstitute and revitalize its central city using European theories of urban design, two features should be noted: how the European vision was modified or compromised, for whatever reasons, and how individual schemes failed to have the larger impact promised, that is, how they failed to catalyze further revitalization.

The ineffective efforts at solving Milwaukee's center city problems suggest that the guiding ideas borrowed from Europe were inadequate to the American context and circumstances and that insufficient attention was paid to other, more dynamic, mechanisms of revitalization. Although this chapter characterizes Milwaukee's early efforts as failure after failure, false start after false start, chapter 3 describes subsequent urban design efforts in Milwaukee in quite another way. In the mid-1970s something happened to end the course of failures and initiate a chain reaction of successes. From our point of view, Milwaukee in the 1970s forgot about European models and found another way to revitalize itself, a distinctively American way. But first, the application of European theory.

FUNCTIONALISM

Functionalist theory offers no specific model for counteracting the problem of suburbanization. We must infer from European practice an approach to keeping residential, retail, and employment concentrations in the center city. The functionalist answer would probably be to make the center city more like suburban developments, with palatable shopping complexes that segregate pedestrian and vehicular traffic and housing that blends urban and suburban amenities. Because land costs in the central city necessitate a high density of population and a concentration of uses, country living is brought into the city in the form of towers in a park or, in the case of employment centers, towers above parking podiums that are made plazalike.

One benefit of recasting the center city in this way is the concomitant renewal that must accompany such extensive restructuring. (In Europe this kind of development was necessitated by war damage; it has only recently been a voluntary reaction to perceived decline and deterioration.) As light, air, and greenery are increased, new structures built, and parking facilitated, outdated, nonfunctional buildings can be replaced. Middle-class occupants can move in to replace the "undesirables" who typically occupy declining urban centers. Functionalist theory does not make clear how large parcels of land are assembled for large-scale restructurings other than through the power of central governments to claim land on behalf of the public good. When that is the method, its high costs are subsidized by those beyond the scope of any given redevelopment project.

The Vision of Towers in a Park

The ideal of functionalist theory, Euro-American style, may be seen in Milwaukee's Juneau Village development, which, once constructed, demonstrated the theory's failure. The development followed in the wake of the federal bulldozers that leveled poor and working-class neighborhoods near downtown so they could be replaced with middle- and upper-income enclaves. To entice the new population group downtown, the functionalist ideal of highrise towers in a parklike setting was chosen, with an adjacent pedestrian-oriented shopping center to offer the amenities of a village and to minimize trips beyond the safety of the enclave.

Functionalist theory argues that because automobiles interfere with human activities, vehicles should be separated from pedestrian areas. In extreme cases this separation means peripheral highways and peripheral parking. In the case of Juneau Village, it meant closing two streets and placing automobiles in underground or structured lots largely masked from public view yet connected to both housing and shopping precincts. The development is located within walking distance of downtown offices. The initial phase included three towers and a shopping center.

Juneau Village was envisioned as a step toward a functionalist revitalization of Milwaukee's downtown. It was not potent enough, how-

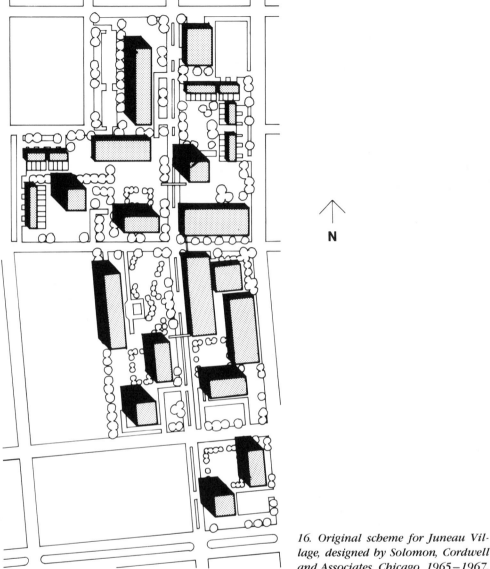

N

16. *Original scheme for Juneau Village, designed by Solomon, Cordwell and Associates, Chicago, 1965–1967.*

ever, to sustain even its own completion, let alone to lead or give impetus. No one seems to have had the necessary conviction to *will* the remainder of the development into being. And, a point we shall stress throughout the chapters that follow, the architecture itself offered no clues to the relation of the development to existing neighborhoods or to the ways succeeding developments should respond to it. The architectural vocabulary was alien to the past and too narrow to guide the future.

As built, the initial stage of Juneau Village was not large enough to restructure its context. Then too, the design was not appealing enough to stimulate a new market of renters or buyers. Although its failure to be realized is most easily blamed on economic conditions and middle-class

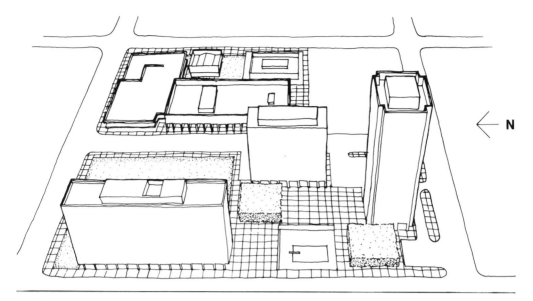

17. *Bird's-eye view of the part of Juneau Village that was actually built.*

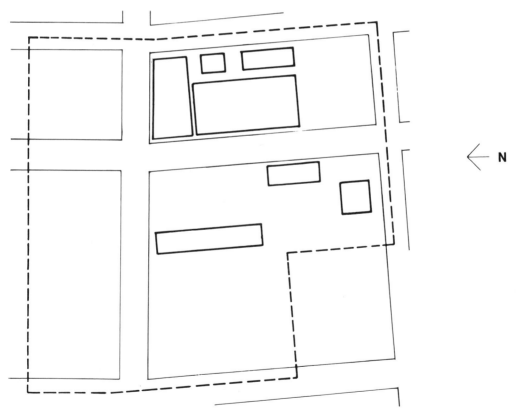

18. *Juneau Village, plan of the section actually built, showing adjacent areas that were cleared as part of the urban renewal effort.*

19. Part of Juneau Village, with shops seen to the right, and part of the site that was used for twenty years for incidental parking.

prejudices, there is another explanation: Juneau Village failed both to recognize its context and to accept a role as catalyst in shaping the character and future of its *American* neighborhood. In short, it was inert, a seed on foreign soil. The transplanted European functionalist vision was not quite right for this American context, nor did it have sufficient conviction to motivate and shape a following.

For years the bulldozed areas around this early stage of Juneau Village lay empty. When it became clear that the village offered no model for subsequent development, pragmatic, visionless alternatives were approved and built in the form of suburban-style garden apartments. That Juneau Village usually is fully occupied testifies not to its actual or conceptual appropriateness or to its potency but to the raw need for housing.

Such transplants of European ideals need not inevitably fail. Our message, which we shall repeat, is that the implanted foreign idea will not succeed on its own merits but must be customized for its American context and must have the power to shape a subsequent context. These processes are discussed in chapter 3.

The Vision of Superblocks

Consolidating elements of the traditional urban plan into superblocks is another feature of functionalist theory. Smaller blocks are joined to form larger ones, and traffic is guided around these. In downtown Milwaukee this treatment was confined to institutions like Marquette University and, in a small way, the Milwaukee School of Engineering, which now spread across former city streets. Such consolidations of institutions across city rights-of-way may be less a product of functionalist thinking than of American campus archetypes, rural groves of academe and academic fortresses walled off from their urban surroundings. But whatever the rationale for creating them, the superblocks in Milwaukee remained isolated instances. They had no significant impact on the shape, character, and fortunes of downtown Milwaukee.

Although superblock strategy was implemented at Juneau Village, where two streets were closed, the area was not restructured in any significant way. Planners of the development specified that pedestrian bridges were to be built to avoid traffic, thus working toward a similar goal of consolidation, but the bridges were not built. Like every other vision imported to restructure downtown Milwaukee, this one was tentative and incomplete and lacked conviction.

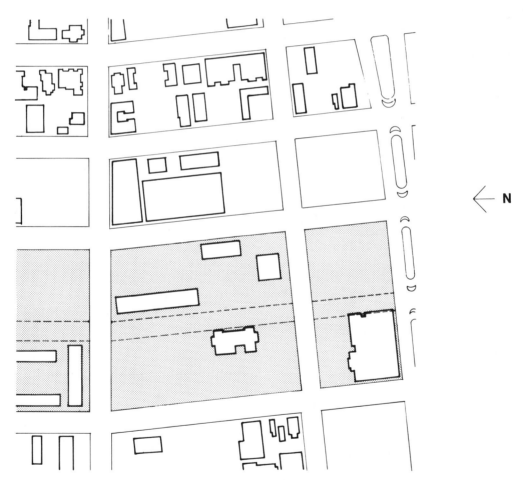

← N

20. *Juneau Village (center and left) and the Milwaukee School of Engineering (right) "superblocks."*

HUMANISM

Humanist thinking appears in isolated and limited instances in American city centers, usually where a single governmental jurisdiction or private developer has had the will and the power to introduce a design in which the quality and pleasure of the immediate human experience are primary concerns. Humanist efforts take three forms, implementing visions of what we call townscape, participation, and heterogeneity.

The Vision of Townscape

Pedestrianized shopping malls that are achieved through street closures have been introduced to make center cities more attractive to pedestrians by wedding the informality of medieval town plazas to the convenience and safety of enclosed suburban shopping complexes. Shopping malls in city centers have been designed to eliminate or restrict vehicular traffic because, it is argued, vehicles compromise the pedestrian experience of the city. The pedestrianized street, like the functionalist urban precinct, was also a European import that in most cases was implemented on American soil without conviction and with little sense of the urban context beyond the individual mall. The early, highly touted, mall on the main street of Fresno, California, failed to have the anticipated impact. It saved the downtown from utter desertion; but it did not revitalize major retail activity in central Fresno. Pedestrian malls in Battle Creek, Michigan, and scores of other cities had even less effect. Nicollet Mall in Minneapolis and Kalamazoo Mall in Kalamazoo, Michigan, by contrast, have been more successful. The difference between Kalamazoo's mall and others, what makes for success, is discussed in chapter 4.

Perhaps the central error of well-meaning public officials and the business community in the many cities where pedestrian malls have failed has been to assume that people want from downtown only convenient parking and a decorated path or, in harsher climates, a sheltered and decorated path. It takes more than basic shelter, low-budget fountains, and "sculpture," however, to transform a dying retail area into an urban place that actually attracts people. Unfortunately, many badly conceived, badly designed, and ineffective Main Street malls litter America. Face-lifting paint-up programs have been similarly unsuccessful in transforming moribund town centers and in radically modifying perceptions and the behavior patterns of consumers. Urbanism does not spring from cosmetics.

Milwaukee's most notable effort toward humanist revitalization has been the reclamation of North Third Street, a collection of turn-of-the-century commercial and industrial structures at the edge of downtown. A two-block area has been both renovated and dressed up. Furniture, like the wooden bench in Figure 22, has been added to make the street seem more hospitable. The result is an area of businesses and offices with an identifiable, visually rich character. Unlike pedestrianized street schemes, Third Street remained open to traffic. Although the area was intended as an initial, catalytic, phase of a reclamation process that would work its

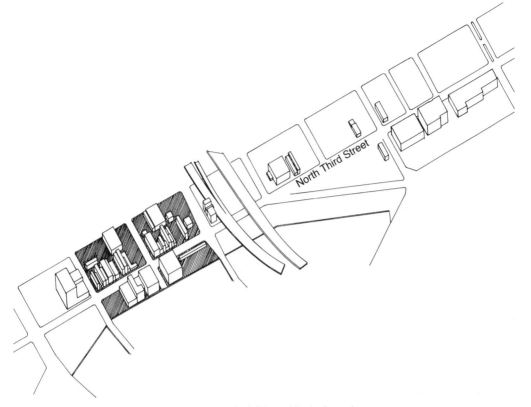

21. North Third Street. The area actually rehabilitated is darkened.

22. The part of North Third Street that was refurbished. Photograph by Paul Pagel.

23. Alfred C. Clas's scheme for developing the edges of the Milwaukee River for public use. The view is to the north. City Hall is to the right of center.

way the entire length of deteriorated Third Street, this was not its effect. Instead, the renovated area stands out as an isolated decorative feature in the cityscape, not as an integral and potent part of the city's life and business.

There is too often, as with Milwaukee's Third Street, an erroneous sense that just doing *something* is enough. But it takes more. Despite the efforts of both the owners and the occupants of the area's buildings, new development did not follow the directions set. A crucial corner lot that should have provided a vivid gateway to the Third Street area is now occupied by a parking lot and an anonymous undersized box of a building. There is no declaration of the area, nothing that marks it as distinct from downtown. The vision for Third Street was not sufficiently compelling; its economics were not impelling; its politics were unwise.

The quality of pedestrians' experience is a persistent concern in humanist thinking. The townscape should be visually satisfying to persons on foot or cycling; pedestrians should "feel at home," feel that they have a place in the city, that they are not alien to it. They should be able to encounter the richness of life as it is actually lived, not single, sanitized, swatches of life.

Milwaukee, like most American cities, did not come to terms with the issue of the pedestrian's experience. This is especially curious since the city and the county have expended considerable resources on parks that enhance pedestrian (and recreational) experiences of nature beyond downtown. But with few exceptions, this commitment does not take the form of a rich and satisfying urban, man-made Milwaukee in the city's core.

Milwaukee's lengthy effort to create riverwalks is a case in point. When the Milwaukee River declined as a focus of commerce and industry, proposals were made to turn it into a European-style amenity with extensive promenades. One of these came from a prominent local architect, Alfred C. Clas. Clas's scheme was not built, however, and instead of a comprehensive, forward-looking program of riverwalk development, only isolated and independent sections appeared, without reference to one another or to an overall vision of riverside pedestrian ways as a humanizing feature.

Following Clas's lead, other architects attempted to revive the idea, but nothing substantial happened. At best, one or two isolated stretches were erected, but without conviction, for they established no link to anything else. In short, they did not acknowledge their context, nor did they realistically anticipate or mold a future.

The Vision of Participation

What we call townscape schemes to rejuvenate Main Street and historic commercial centers are but one aspect of humanist concern. Another, in which the United States, in some ways, is further ahead than Europe, is to involve people in the molding of their own environments. Home ownership is more usual in America than in Europe; do-it-yourself modifications are a concomitant pleasure. Americans seem to have a greater choice of places to live and ways to live. In this sense, "nesting" and "making places" are quite widespread in America.

Yet as construction and financing costs have risen, the choices have become narrower, those able to make them fewer. And more to our point, personal involvement in shaping environments is restricted to home turf. The character of the center city is usually the province of public bureaucracies, developers, and financing institutions. Although citizens can try to take charge of center city areas through neighborhood action groups, these groups typically have little power.

The preservation of historic areas and neighborhoods, another European idea imported to America, is possibly the most successful of the imports. But only what already exists can be preserved; preservation allows no shaping of new neighborhoods and new city centers.

Milwaukee's other efforts to mold areas near downtown have been well-meaning but far from noteworthy. For years reclamation of the old warehouse district south of downtown was discussed, and a few individuals risked time and money in renovating and adapting a few buildings for new uses. These efforts did not turn the tide, however, nor did they precipitate widespread action by others. Efforts by merchants east of the river in downtown Milwaukee were similarly ineffective. Fearful of declining sales, the merchants formed an association that erected plaques to identify East Town as a distinctive part of downtown. The plaques, however, could not save East Town's one department store, which was closed and was razed.

With few exceptions the humanist ideals of making the city visually pleasing and physically congenial and of encouraging people to mold their environments according to their own visions have not blossomed in American center cities. San Francisco offers one of the few exceptions. The Embarcadero Center and Golden Gateway development there intertwine office, retail, and housing uses with satisfying pedestrian areas that are offered not grudgingly but with determination. Nearby, residents of Telegraph Hill have banded together to protect their neighborhood from exploitation and defilement. But San Francisco's experience is atypical. In Milwaukee such efforts had little effect.

The Vision of Heterogeneity

A third element of humanist theory, beyond townscape aesthetics and citizen participation, is the conviction that heterogeneity is a positive feature of urbanism, that homogeneity dulls and stultifies. American urban designers and planners typically adopt this view but usually fail to implement it. For example, the functionalist predilection to separate land uses compromises the humanist vision of a visually rich and socially diverse city center. Even though a variety of uses may be outlined for downtown, too often office buildings are carefully removed from housing, institutions from commercial use. In recent years this error has been corrected in some cities, where mixed use is not only allowed but encouraged within buildings and complexes. More than a mixture, however, *mixing* is needed, truly integrated zones of transition where land uses and activities actually overlap. This notion is not original; it is a feature of most rewarding urban centers. Yet it is too seldom a conscious objective in revitalization plans.

Although Milwaukee is showing signs of moving toward a greater mix in the city center, a recent zoning scheme for downtown insists on separating commercial, office, and other uses. While the downtown itself will be heterogeneous, no one part of it will be. Granted, the absence of zoning could be damaging. But transitional zoning between designated land use areas would encourage the mixings that are so important to satisfying urbanism.

The dearth of humanist urban design in an American city born of nineteenth-century circumstances is perhaps not surprising. Culturally and socially, cities like Milwaukee have been mixing (not melting) pots in which the fear of others and a perceived need to protect what one has have been primary motivations in personal, corporate, and civic decision making. Then, too, the people who immigrated to work in America's emerging industrial cities brought with them little in the way of positive urban experience. Perhaps only after several generations could these immigrant Americans overcome anti-urban prejudices and evolve to a point where a thoughtful design of the urban place was not a luxury but a reflex action.

Milwaukee does have some design achievements: City Hall, the old Federal Building, Lake Park, and numerous churches testify to taste and commitment in design. But these isolated achievements do not add up to the humanist vision of a rewarding townscape, broad involvement in decision making, and a social and cultural mix.

SYSTEMIC DESIGN

Whereas European theorists proposed that both movement through the city and building production be systematized, and even coordinated, American systemic thinking has been focused almost exclusively on expressways and rapid transit. Efforts like Operation Breakthrough, a federal program of the 1970s that sought to encourage mass-production methods for housing, had no noticeable impact on the character of the city. The hope of the Dutch structuralists that people might fashion their own homes within a broadly supportive communal structure was not answered; the penchant for do-it-yourself projects around the house is hardly equivalent. Thus to speak of urban systems in America means, for the most part, to speak of traffic plans.

Edmund Bacon's recommendations for Philadelphia demonstrate how the systemic approach can be applied to an American city. Bacon asserts that to influence future development, urban designers "must have a clear concept of the underlying design structure that must be produced to set in motion the involved processes of city-building." He recommends an "underlying order" of "simultaneous movement systems" conceived three-dimensionally. Movement systems become "a dominant organizing force in architectural design." Distinctions between speeds and modes of movement need to be acknowledged and, in fact, capitalized upon.[7] In short, the movement system is conceived as "an abstract design, from which the design structure of the city begins to emerge." The places where different movement modes connect should be marked by "special emphasis and design enrichment."[8]

Land and movement in Milwaukee, as in so many American cities, are organized by a uniform street grid. The two exceptions to the overall scheme are the radial streets that remain as vestiges of intercity travel before the construction of freeways (Chicago Avenue, Fond du Lac Avenue, Green Bay Avenue, and so forth) and a grid of arterials at one-mile intervals that have been widened to concentrate and facilitate vehicular movement at higher speeds.

The Vision of Express Traffic

The most obvious evidence of systemic thinking in Milwaukee, as in most American cities, is the expressway system. It was designed to circumscribe downtown and, superficially, to follow a Gruen-like vision of a central core surrounded by parking lots that intervene between high-speed roads and a pedestrianized city center. A closer look reveals that neither element of the design was realized in Milwaukee. For one thing, the circumferential expressway was not completed. (In the course of construction it ran into humanist values in the form of neighborhood opposition.) Further, with two exceptions, parking structures were not built adjacent

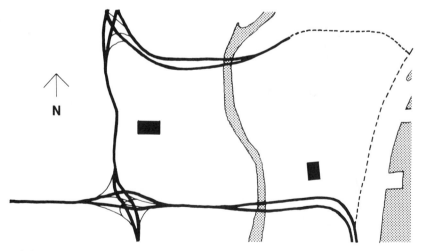

24. The intended expressway system loop and two somewhat related parking structures (darkened). Broken lines indicate sections left unconstructed.

to the high-speed trafficways but appeared on scattered sites throughout downtown, thus assuring rather than eliminating confrontations between vehicles and pedestrians. Although systemic thinking appears to have been the most successful of the four orientations in urban design theory employed in restructuring downtown Milwaukee, the scope of its application (part of an expressway loop with two associated parking structures) was limited. This vision touched only one of several urban systems, and that one incompletely. Other American cities had parallel experiences in pursuing a narrow systemic vision of rationalized vehicular access and similarly ran into opposition from citizens with a broader range of concerns and values. Expressway construction in San Francisco and New Orleans also was stopped.

The Vision of Efficient Transit

Systemic theorists try to rationalize public transit in city centers by integrating various traffic modes (rapid transit systems in Chicago, Washington, D.C., and San Francisco align at times with expressways) and (as in Toronto) by concentrating the development of new buildings near points of access to public transportation systems. In the multi-nucleated cities of the American Southwest new office/commercial centers are being built at the intersection of freeways (in Houston and Dallas, for example). Elsewhere, railroad rights-of-way are being reclaimed for public transport use. Streetcars, buses, and rapid transit trains intersect along San Francisco's Market Street. Although these transportation systems can restructure a city, in most cities where they are constructed they represent limited solutions and have no broad impact. Systemic theory demands a more comprehensive approach. It proposes a restructuring of the city that improves not only mass transit but housing and other urban functions too by having a coherent, flexible, and extensive armature that responds to a wide range of needs and uses. Although Milwaukee periodically talked about such programs, it did nothing.

FORMALISM

Formalism, whether Beaux-Arts or neo-rationalist, assumes that there are archetypal patterns and configurations with universal significance from which urban design should be drawn. Although the emphases and the socio-economic effects of the two approaches differ dramatically—proponents of Beaux-Arts formalism stressed axial organization and static spaces and, more recently, proponents of neo-rationalist formalism have focused on a finer and more circumstantial urban grain—both points of view assume that urban form is best drawn from timeless patterns. Neo-rationalism is now stronger than Beaux-Arts formalism as an intellectual current, but it has had little impact in America to date because the important Italian treatises of the 1960s that formulated it were not translated for a decade. Further, neo-rationalist theory is strongly related to historical European urban patterns and therefore is difficult to transpose to American contexts.

Aldo Rossi, a key advocate of neo-rationalism, speaks approvingly of the typical American grid, though he does not indicate what one could do with it or how it might guide and give impetus to contemporary urban form. Rossi speaks approvingly, too, of American towns with what might be called a late-medieval character, towns like Boston and Nantucket. But again, Rossi does not indicate how these models could inform new urban patterns. The scale of building in Manhattan impressed Rossi, but should other American cities seek to achieve the character of Manhattan? Because neo-rationalism has had little impact to date, the study of formalist efforts in American cities must focus on Beaux-Arts City Beautiful schemes. But we are convinced that the points we make here about earlier Beaux-Arts formalism will apply when neo-rationalist formalism appears in American streets: it will fail to blossom because it too is narrow and alien.

The Vision of Civic Axis

The grandest plan to put Beaux-Arts formalism into practice in Milwaukee envisioned a civic axis rising at a domed county courthouse. A broad avenue would unfold between flanking gardens and then pause at a *rond point* braced by four buildings of civic significance. Finally the axis

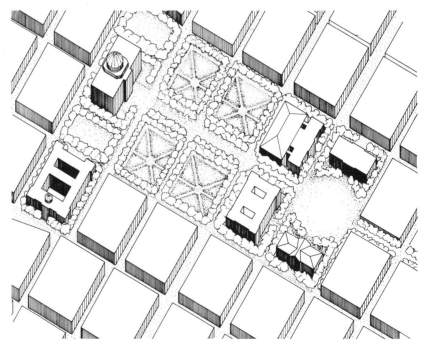

25. A drawing suggesting Alfred C. Clas's scheme for a Milwaukee Civic Center.

26. Milwaukee County Courthouse seen down the "civic axis" of Kilbourn Avenue. Buildings along the axis have not been sympathetic to the concept. The bridge connecting the convention center and auditorium indicates how little the idea of a civic axis meant to a subsequent generation.

would cross the Milwaukee River and terminate at the portals of the preexisting muscular City Hall. Of this grand but feasible vision (after all, San Francisco had managed to build the beginnings of such a dream), only a courthouse (and then not a domed one) was built.

Milwaukee made a second effort to achieve a monumental civic axis, with the County Courthouse as an anchor for Kilbourn Avenue, which extended toward City Hall but angled off to miss that monument and passed on to terminate at the bluff above Lake Michigan. Civic buildings and other edifices of substance were to line this grand avenue. This second effort, however, akin to Edmund Bacon's idea for a "shaft of space" (outlined in *The Design of Cities*), either was too grand for the city's civic and financial resources or, perhaps, was begun too late. The Beaux-Arts inspired City Beautiful movement, which sought to link American cities to the archetypal grandeur of European capitals, was losing potency in America at the time the construction of the Milwaukee County Courthouse was completed. Few of the structures built along Kilbourn Avenue fulfilled the original magnificent idea, and what has been built for the most part does not reinforce the sense of a civic axis. The Performing Arts Center, for example, although it was built on Kilbourn Avenue, does not front that axis but rather a minor, competing axis, the Milwaukee River. Kilbourn Avenue was simply too long; Milwaukee did not have enough civic energy to realize the conception. This was another case where the imported vision did not suit the realities.

The Vision of Public Realm

The shared, public, realm of a city often takes the shape of public squares or patches of nature in the city. Neither archetype seems to have inspired design decisions in Milwaukee when in recent years a new riverside park was created downtown. At best Pere Marquette Park is an amenity offering places to sit and stroll, but it is a compromise. It is neither an urban square nor an area given over to another, un-urban, world of nature. It does not pull parts of the city together; instead it does little more than occupy a landscaped area between other, unrelated, areas. Suburban lawns seem to have inspired it. Like so many other efforts to do something in downtown Milwaukee, this one lacked both conviction and a vivid guiding vision.

Elsewhere downtown the redevelopment of formal green squares, like Cathedral Square and Zeidler Park, has accentuated neither their urban nor their natural character. They have none of the suggestiveness of an eighteenth-century London square, for example, or a lush Victorian urban garden. These efforts failed not for having roots in European theory but for having no roots at all.

27. Pere Marquette Park, situated downtown on the Milwaukee River, which was once used for commerce, commemorates the landing of the missionary-explorer Father Marquette. The site is prime in every way. It marks the important historical process of exploration. It faces the Performing Arts Center across the river and has frontage along the Kilbourn Avenue civic axis. It offers diagonal views of downtown and of Milwaukee's striking City Hall. It is a crossroads for civic, commercial, industrial, and sporting Milwaukee as well as a gateway to North Third Street, with its Victorian buildings. The rich, strategic, and meaningful nature of the site was ignored or suppressed, however, in a design that features a suburban lawn, a curving walk, and some standard benches.

28. *Interior, Plankinton Arcade. Holabird and Roche, architects, Chicago, 1916. Bridges and dome highlight the intersection of the building's axes. The longer one parallels Wisconsin Avenue.*

The Vision of Galleria

The Plankinton Arcade was Milwaukee's version of a classic urban element, the spacious skylighted semipublic commercial interior whose precedents range from Milan's Galleria and London's Burlington Arcade to more modest manifestations in Cleveland and Providence. Once a lively place, the Plankinton Arcade was allowed to age and decline. For more than sixty years it remained an isolated good idea, with no influence on its context. No one seems to have been inspired enough by it to copy or improve upon it or to link up with it—not, that is, until the mid-1970s.

PRAGMATISM

Although one finds in a city like Milwaukee evidence of each urban design theory originating in Europe, none of the theories seems to have worked powerfully. None has proven strong enough to exert a substantial influence. The failures of European theory in Milwaukee can be attributed to (1) the inappropriateness of specific models in the American context, (2) a lack of conviction, (3) a concern with too few factors affecting urban development, and (4) the attitude that each new development effort is independent of its context. Urban design in Milwaukee *does* seem to have been guided by a collection of loosely held imported ideas and a decision-making process that boils down to pragmatism. Even in Milwaukee's heyday of socialist idealism, what was sought was not a vital, shared urbanism but better sewers.

Whereas theories about new possibilities for center cities often play a central role in European efforts toward revitalization, in America they typically do not. At best, American efforts include gestures toward ideas halfheartedly borrowed. In Europe one finds classic experiments with humanist, functionalist, systemic and formalist urban design; in America one usually finds only clouded versions of those ideas.

This is not to say that theory is entirely absent from American urban design projects but only that it seldom impels them. For every scheme like Bacon's plan for reconstituting Philadelphia, or Baltimore's renaissance, or Rockefeller Center, there are twenty that rise not from a vision but from conventions, or hopes of making a quick killing, or external pressures. Typically, American schemes respond not to the ideological questions What should be done? and What is right? but to the practical questions What has to be done? (politically, economically, socially), What can be done? (economically and politically), and Who benefits? (economically, politically, socially).

American urban revitalization is characterized by pragmatism, a concern with practical and feasible consequences. Perhaps nothing makes this point better than Jonathan Barnett's textbook *An Introduction to Urban Design,* a virtual bible of urban design in America. He calls it a "methodology" for dealing with the accelerated pace of change that characterizes our times.[9] Chapters identify three key forces to be contended with (ecological concerns, community participation, and historic preservation) and the leverage that can be applied to direct design and development. But he carefully avoids prescribing goals toward which the leverage and the forces might be applied. He does not propose what should be but does tell how to achieve particular ends. He subscribes to the view that people should decide for themselves, that there is no one best ideal for urban design.

We are sympathetic and probably more like Barnett than unlike him in avoiding prescription, a preference for certain solutions toward which all urban design schemes should be aimed. We are sympathetic in particular with his recommendation that urban designers offer not specific designs or abstract policies but *rules* to guide choices.[10] But surely someone needs to take the lead in precipitating hopes and communicating visions for the urban place in America, hopes and visions that are more than merely workable.

There are several obvious reasons for the tendency of American urban design to be pragmatic rather than idealist, pedestrian rather than inspiring. First, most Americans have little experience with potent, positive, personally rewarding urbanism. (One urban designer confides that "if the City Council or Redevelopment Agency members haven't been to London or Rome, we as designers know we have an uphill battle!") Second, many American towns and cities were mapped out strictly as money-making enterprises. The goals in their settlement were ease in legally describing parcels and the greatest possible profit from real estate sales and investments. (Whereas the nineteenth century envisioned urban development as selling off parcels of land, the mid-twentieth century has seen it as an investment that one can write off or that will pay off.) As a consequence, the typical American urban pattern is a grid that from its inception did not respond to the physical setting but facilitated surveying, easy sales, and access to transportation. The understanding of land as a commodity the individual can own and exploit pervades American culture; it does not, unfortunately, create a dependable basis for good urban design.

Third, most American towns do not have the long history that imbues cities with richness and depth; few have had the chance European cities have had to be overlaid, modified, and amended. Aldo Rossi claims that American cities are as evocative as European ones, but those he likes—Nantucket, Providence, Boston—are not typically American in their formulation but are more typical of Europe, the products of late medieval life, thought, and economy. Few American cities are as obviously cities of distinguishable parts as these.[11]

Finally, Americans have tended to idealize nature and the experience of nature rather than to idealize the city and the experience of urbanism and civitas. In this prejudice we have a considerable tradition—in the writings of Thomas Jefferson, Henry David Thoreau, Ralph Waldo Emerson, and, more recently, Frank Lloyd Wright. Even now, though a few advocates of urbanism sing the virtues of the city, Americans move to the suburbs. This anti-urban bias is declining, especially in cities where gentrification has been possible and has been promoted and made profitable. Time gradually will lend the American town a sense of history, of one era overlaid on another and another. Because this has not happened yet, however, Americans, unless they live on the Eastern Seaboard or in isolated cities like San Francisco and New Orleans, expect little of their cities and find little there beyond economic reward. No wonder they tend to be pragmatic in deciding the future of their towns and cities. Nor is it any wonder that the task of urban designers in America is as much to educate and to raise aspirations as it is to design and plan strategies.

Although it would be handy to characterize American pragmatism as something like European functionalism, they are not alike. American pragmatism evidences none of the idealism of European functionalism. Furthermore, pragmatic Americans pick and choose as though theories could be selected à la carte. Whereas a European functionalist scheme would eschew sentimental historicizing references to the past that characterize humanism and a formalist scheme would not tolerate an overriding and extensive, systemic, pattern for everything, pragmatic Americans willingly mix ideas, not because they are convinced of the worth of the related theories but because those ingredients appear to be called for. Although eclectic mixes can be rich, they are not necessarily so. The key to a satisfying eclecticism is a knowledgeable and sensitive chef d'oeuvre and a good recipe book.

American pragmatism has drawbacks, but its virtue may well be its low regard for narrow theories. Existing theories are exclusionist; that is, they ignore some factors to build a strong, singleminded case for others. A humanist scheme, for example, neglects economic issues; functionalist schemes typically ignore the importance of cultural traditions; systemic schemes are overbearing and too optimistic about technology; formalist schemes assume that Europe had all the right and sufficient answers by the nineteenth century.

The disadvantage of American pragmatism, apart from the uncertainty about what will emerge from any given mix, is that it leads to urban design that envisions no better world. Even if such schemes work, they arouse no enthusiasm; or if they do, the arousal is temporary. Of most concern, pragmatic, happenstance approaches to urban design fail to provide a direction for subsequent development efforts.

A respected urban designer practicing in an American city asks the reasonable question, "Is a theory of urban design for America necessary? Isn't it enough to work intuitively from one's experience of good and bad urban design?" Our answer is that working from theory provides both a discipline and a basis for evaluation. It provides a reference point to which one can return in making decisions. And it provides a standard against which decisions can be measured. Without this external discipline and standard, there are two serious dangers. First, decisions may be made not with reference to goals but in response to local or momentary pressures. A design becomes the product of miscellaneous demands (economize, satisfy that alderman, don't antagonize the newspapers, maximize off-street parking, make snow removal easy, and so forth) rather than larger goals. Second, miscellaneous decisions can cancel out each other and leave little of significance as an end product. We can imagine Milwaukee's Pere Marquette Park resulting from a collection of decisions, each of which is justifiable but which collectively add up to neither an urban park nor an urban place: plant grass, minimize low shrubs, offer benches, discourage loitering, make it natural, permit surveillance, orient toward the Performing Arts Center, make a front yard for the County Historical Center, curve the paths, facilitate maintenance, provide street lights, and so on. At the larger scale, decisions made for one district cancel out decisions made in another; the parts of a city do not reinforce one another. Although theory can be misused, without it, little will be achieved that is significant and memorable.

Although we feel too distant from European needs and circumstances to evaluate the relation between theory and practice in that context, we do feel qualified to examine and prescribe for American circumstances. American cities and towns can be revitalized only if the following premises apply to the native predilection for pragmatism:

1. The time scale of revitalization must be longer than the five or ten years of a financial balance sheet. Renewal must have within it the ingredients of its own subsequent regeneration.

2. A good urban center is more than an efficient machine for producing wealth. It has a civic dimension as well. Civic pride and personal identification with the city can have a deep long-range impact that does not appear readily in an economic forecast or in tallies of vehicles satisfactorily channeled and stored.

3. A vital urban center is not a suburban shopping center inserted downtown. It is more complex and less time-bound. (We like the concept of sedimentation,[12] the idea that the good city center is layered by time.)

4. Architecture is not the process of merely decorating cities. That the world's great cities are also the seats of the world's great architecture is not accidental. Architecture and urbanism are part of the same attitude.

5. Specific visions are needed to guide urban design, and these will vary from locale to locale.

American pragmatism is attractive as a method of urban design insofar as it is not exclusive and doctrinaire or limited and narrow as a result of being dialectically opposed to something else. An absence of aspirations other than profit, however, and the use of stock, borrowed approaches and ingredients restrict the achievement of American urban design.

Even though no one factor will correct the shortcomings of existing urban design methods and models, new ideas and theories can turn the process in more promising directions. For example, the involvement of citizens in decision making promises to increase the concern for quality as well as for economic feasibility. But because most Americans have so little experience of positive urbanism, they are hard-pressed to direct the process well.

Another new direction is to pay attention to the chemistry of urban design, the way elements act upon and interact with one another. The chemistry of investment and dividends is well known and relatively dependable, but the chemistry of social and architectural elements in urban design needs greater attention and understanding. In this interaction we see a specifically American approach, a chain reaction that links private and public initiative not in pursuit of a singular master plan but in an ongoing process of action and reaction that is always moderated but never completely controlled. Just such a chemistry of urban revitalization is the subject of chapter 3.

3

THE CONCEPT OF URBAN CATALYSTS

As we argued in the preceding chapter, the changing stances in European urban design theory in the past few decades have offered inadequate guidance for American cities. In particular, existing urban design theories do not indicate how to achieve the goals associated with them in an American context. Perhaps because of their origins, most of the theories seem to assume a central government with the political and economic power to implement the development envisioned. In the United States such an assumption is not justified except when federal programs like urban renewal or Operation Breakthrough or the Interstate Highway System or urban homesteading appear. But federal programs cannot be counted on to support urban design efforts consistently and should not form the basis of urban design theory for America. At most, the urban designer can use federal programs occasionally, at particular times and in specific situations.

American designers and developers have often tried to implement aspects of these European visions by using American political and financing tools, including tax increment financing (the tax on increased land value), municipal write-offs of land acquisition costs, tax deferrals, tax abatements, mortgage guarantees, profit sharing, incentive zoning, and so forth. Nonetheless, American urban design typically lacks appropriate, American, visions of cities. In short, European theories offer ideals of limited applicability and few tools for implementing them. Pragmatic America offers a changing set of tools but no theory appropriate for America. We need a different way of looking at the problem of reconstituting America's center cities, a different vision.

We do not argue with existing European-based concepts; in fact, we recommend, pragmatically, adopting many European urban values. But note: it is the *values,* not the forms associated with them, that we commend. The following values derived from European cities and European-based urban design theories constitute the givens of good urbanism, not only in Europe but in America:

1. Mixed activities are basic to cities.
2. Buildings (and the spaces they form) are the natural increments of urban growth.

3. New urban growth must recognize the context provided by past construction.

4. A major goal of urban design is the shaping of public open space, including meaningful street space.

5. Streets must accommodate various forms of transit and enhance pedestrian activity and movement.

6. Transportation systems should be rational.

7. Urban places should be varied to enhance the activities associated with them: housing, neighborhood shopping, major retail, civic, and so forth.

8. Citizens should have a role in shaping urban settings.

But even as we commend the values, we diverge sharply from the tenets of both European idealism and American pragmatism in considering how to implement urban design ideas. We suggest that urban design for center cities, instead of being conceived as the process of implementing one or another ideal image of the city, using various available tools, is more appropriately thought of as a process of arranging catalytic reactions. There should be no ultimate vision for the urban center, either functionalist, humanist, systemic, or formalist. And a tool box of implementation techniques should not simply be left open for use anywhere at any time. Rather, there should be *a sequence of limited, achievable visions, each with the power to kindle and condition other achievable visions.* This would be urban catalysis. Visions for the new urban center should be modest and incremental, but their impact should be substantial, in contrast to the large visions that have been the rule, with their minimal or catastrophic impact.

The metaphors guiding urban design theory to date have been inadequate. Organismic and mechanical metaphors ("heart of the city," "the city is a tree—or semilattice," "organism," "mechanism") are of limited use as guides to architectural and urban design decisions. We find the chemical/catalytic analogy to be more useful and versatile. An urban catalyst might be a hotel in one city, a shopping complex in another, a transportation hub in a third. It could be a museum or theater. It could be a designed open space or, at the smallest scale, a special feature like a colonnade or a fountain.

An urban catalyst has a greater purpose than to solve a functional problem, or create an investment, or provide an amenity. A catalyst is an urban element that is shaped by the city (its "laboratory" setting) and then, in turn, shapes its context. *Its purpose is the incremental, continuous regeneration of the urban fabric. The important point is that the catalyst is not a single end product but an element that impels and guides subsequent development.*

Urban catalysts are dynamic; they act and have effects. In contrast, functionalist architecture may be conceived as a physical model for cities; humanist design, as a stimulating setting for human activities; systemic design, as a network of communication; and formalist design, as an embodiment of urban archetypes. Each one has a limited scope and vision. Each suggests that cities should have a single underlying nature. By contrast, urban catalysts are capable of molding a city in any of several ways, none of them dictated by a single-minded vision.

Though the metaphorical use of the word *catalyst* is widespread in urban design and planning literature, the concept of urban catalysis has value beyond the suggestiveness of the metaphor; in fact there is an analogy between the chemical process of catalysis and mechanisms of successful urban design and urbanism. Often those who talk about catalysts refer to vast developments—Gruen's Fort Worth Plan and Pei's Boston Government Center plan were intended as catalysts; but we propose that urban catalysts are better thought of as smaller elements—a building, a fragment of a building, a complex of buildings, or even a report or set of guidelines. Although renewal and revitalization schemes for cities are often touted as catalysts, many of these schemes remain inert and have little impact. They do not cause the promised urban reactive change. Sometimes the term *catalyst* refers to economic processes, typically an infusion of funds that leads to other infusions of funds, or, at a gross scale, it means that one development makes additional developmental projects look like good investment risks. Mere change, however, just adding development to development, does not assure good design or rewarding urbanism, nor do mere investments in redevelopment, as countless renewal schemes demonstrate.

The subtleties of the catalytic concept and its power to help us understand the interaction of urban design and other factors are usually overlooked. Architecture, too, is catalytic. Not only infusions of capital that incidentally produce new buildings and reconstructed streets but buildings themselves can be catalysts, ensuring the high quality of urban redevelopment. Urban design *quality* is determined at the scale of buildings, not balance sheets.

Catalysis involves the introduction of one ingredient to modify others. In the process, the catalyst sometimes remains intact and sometimes is itself modified. Adapted to describe the urban design process, catalysis may be characterized as follows:

1. The introduction of a new element (the catalyst) causes a reaction that modifies existing elements in an area. Although most often thought of as economic (investments beget investments), catalysts can also be social, legal, political, or—and this is our point—architectural. The potential of a building to influence other buildings, to lead urban design, is enormous.

2. Existing urban elements of value are enhanced or transformed in positive ways. The new need not obliterate or devalue the old but can redeem it.

3. The catalytic reaction is contained; it does not damage its context. To unleash a force is not enough. Its impact must be channeled.

4. To ensure a positive, desired, predictable catalytic reaction, the ingredients must be considered, understood, and accepted. (Note the para-

dox: a comprehensive understanding is needed to produce a good limited effect.) Cities differ; urban design cannot assume uniformity.

5. The chemistry of all catalytic reactions is not predetermined; no single formula can be specified for all circumstances.

6. Catalytic design is strategic. Change occurs not from simple intervention but through careful calculation to influence future urban form step by step. (Again, a paradox: no one recipe for successful urban catalysis exists, yet each catalytic reaction needs a strategic recipe.)

7. A product better than the sum of the ingredients is the goal of each catalytic reaction. Instead of a city of isolated pieces, imagine a city of wholes.

8. The catalyst need not be consumed in the process but can remain identifiable. Its identity need not be sacrificed when it becomes part of a larger whole. The persistence of individual identities—many owners, occupants, and architects—enriches the city.

Existing theories specify desirable but narrow ends: a meaningful public realm; or efficient and coherent organization; or personal, experiential, gratification. They do not indicate either how these ends can be achieved or that all of them have merit. At best, implementation is described in generalities: citizen participation, collective (rather than individual) investment, poetic transformation, administrative fiat, and so forth.

A catalytic theory of urban design is not an alternative to existing theories but subsumes them, accepting what they have to offer. What it does that existing theories fail to do satisfactorily is describe how to get from

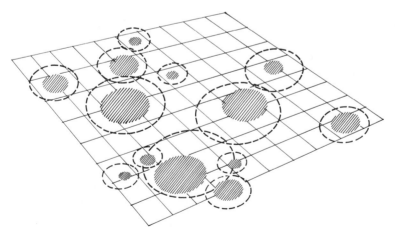

29. Diagrammatic representation of the catalytic process. Actions (represented by hatching), whether developments, restorations, reports, or whatever, catalyze other actions, which in turn lend impetus to others. Each action is constrained too, so that the reaction does not destroy the city. The moderating aspect of the process is represented by the broken lines around the hatching.

goals to implementation. Action and reaction, cause and effect are integral to the catalytic concept.

Catalytic theory does not prescribe a single mechanism of implementation, a final form, or a preferred visual character for all urban areas. Rather, it prescribes an essential feature for urban developments: the power to kindle other action. The focus is the interaction of new and existing elements and their impact on future urban form, not the approximation of a preordained physical ideal.

To explain the concept of urban catalysis in more concrete terms, we look at events in Milwaukee's downtown, in particular, the impact of a new setting for retail activity called the Grand Avenue. Milwaukee is an appropriate case study because its downtown had been declining for more than a decade. The urban center was not just inert but entropic, having dropped to fourteenth among the fourteen shopping centers in the region. The Grand Avenue quickly became the region's prime retail center, and both downtown itself and attitudes about downtown changed dramatically. The changes are not the by-product of new stimuli; there are no new factories, no mammoth construction projects, no growth industries pumping money into the local economy. Instead, the changes are the product of thoughtful strategic planning and a commitment to design quality. After this chapter looks in detail at catalytic events in Milwaukee, examples of the catalytic urban design process in other cities are discussed in chapter 4.

Until 1973, the revitalization of downtown Milwaukee was little more than sputterings, false starts, isolated and improbable visions, and a broad conviction that "it can't happen here." Land was cleared for a functionalist urban enclave (Juneau Village), only one-third of which was built. A downtown freeway loop, begun but never finished, did not satisfy the desirable (systemic) objective of linking a series of parking structures to freeways. A civic axis, inaugurated with the design for the County Courthouse, dissipated almost immediately. Incidental historic reclamations were undertaken, but they did not exert a potent influence on other developments; as a result, there was little sense of historical downtown Milwaukee. New highrise office structures rose, conceived, however, not as integral parts of a revived downtown but as objects on private plazas/podiums.

Warnings that downtown was dying had gone out as early as 1957, when Milwaukee's Board of Public Land Commissioners declared that "the vitality of the central district is threatened," and everyone believed them. What was wrong in Milwaukee was, first, attitude, a lack of will to make things happen; second, isolated rather than integrated redevelopment—revitalization efforts lacked coordinated direction; third, the absence of effective centralized power. City Hall could not revitalize the city, nor could individual corporations.

To turn Milwaukee around required a combination of corporate commitment to the city (above and beyond immediate corporate profits) and a political structure willing to support this private initiative in a variety of ways. This is not to say that corporate Milwaukee took control; rather, it provided the focused economic and political means that could become a driving force for redevelopment. Years of miscellaneous federal, municipal, and private investment had failed to reverse the decline of the center city. Such a reversal required "a more comprehensive and continuous approach to new development—a leveraging of public and private investment in synergistic efforts." The use of corporate funds at such a scale in the traditionally public realm of development planning was new and, as is so often argued, brought a needed sense of businessmindedness. "Corporate funding of planning replaces some municipal funds . . . , but it does not usurp public responsibility or involvement."[1] A partnership of public and private interests is built.

The story of catalytic redevelopment in Milwaukee begins with a 1973 study commissioned by the Greater Milwaukee Committee. It offered a vision for a new downtown, which in turn could change attitudes. The Chicago office of Skidmore Owings and Merrill prepared the report, called "Milwaukee Central Area Study." It recommended the formation of a development corporation and the creation of a retail core with related uses.

Catalytic processes in Milwaukee began when the SOM study aroused corporate and municipal interest. This combination had the potential to attract a third element, a developer, the Rouse Company, to manage the process. According to a Rouse representative, "What we look for in rebuilding is a once vibrant area with a strong current business and civic commitment to improvement." Milwaukee now had that.[2]

When it became clear that risk capital would be needed for renewal to occur in downtown Milwaukee, the Milwaukee Redevelopment Corporation (MRC) was created. Its first, crucial, project was to remold and reshape the image of downtown. The vehicle would be an innovative center city shopping complex incorporating the best features of suburban shopping complexes with the vitality and richness of an urban center.

The Milwaukee Redevelopment Corporation then took three steps. First, it proposed the construction of a retail complex called the Grand Avenue, which would both recall Grand Avenue, Milwaukee's historical retail/commercial artery (now Wisconsin Avenue), and offer an interior place, a semipublic realm better than that found in any suburban shopping center. Second, the MRC listened and responded to reactions to the idea. Third, it became a leading partner in the development and a link between private and public interests and investments in the project.

What is the secret of the Grand Avenue's success? "A bold vision, the money to turn a vision into reality, and the willingness of government and business leaders to work toward a common goal are important ingredients." From the point of view of former MRC Executive Director Stephen Dragos, "What ultimately made the Grand Avenue more than just an architect's sketch was the muscle provided by city and business leaders. That they recognized the need for such a venture and believed in it enough to gain widespread support made the Grand Avenue a reality."[3] Henry Maier, for example, the city's mayor, and Francis Ferguson, head of the Northwestern Mutual Life Insurance Company, "moved heaven and

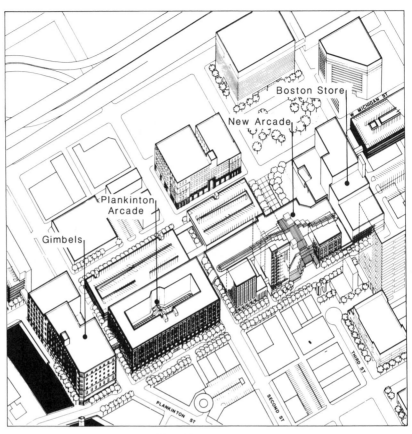

Site From North

North

0   100   300

30. *The Grand Avenue, Milwaukee. After a study in 1970 indicated that Milwaukee needed risk capital for renewal, the Milwaukee Redevelopment Corporation (MRC) was formed in 1973 as a limited-profit, blue-chip grouping of large firms. Conceived by the MRC and the city in 1976, the Grand Avenue concept was reviewed in 1977, and negotiations with a developer, the Rouse Company, began in 1978. Private investment amounted to $18 million, with the Rouse Company contributing $19.5 million. The $39-million investment of the city of Milwaukee took the form of an Urban Development Action Grant and a tax-increment bond issue. No new tax dollars were involved.*

a. Aerial view, looking south, shows how the Grand Avenue links the two existing department stores at either end and incorporates the existing Plankinton Arcade building. The tall buildings above Boston Store in this view predate the construction of the Grand Avenue.

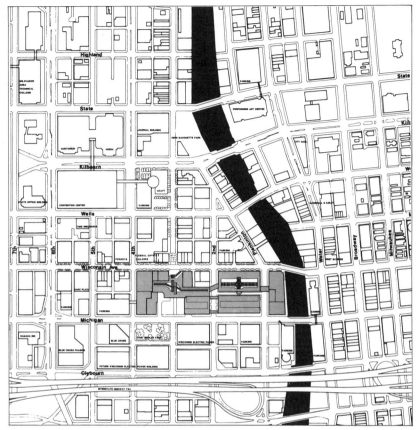

Downtown Milwaukee

North

0   200   600

b. The scale of the Grand Avenue development is evident in this plan of down-town Milwaukee.

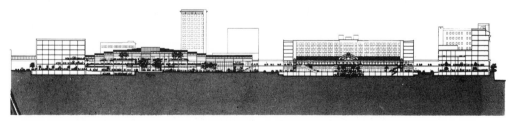

c. This section through the Grand Avenue looks north, showing the department stores anchoring each end and the two major interior spaces—a new one (left) and the existing Plankinton Arcade.

LEGEND
1. WEST OF DOWNTOWN
2. EXTENSION OF THE GRAND AVENUE
3. THE GRAND AVENUE
4. HYATT HOTEL AND FEDERAL PLAZA
5. RIVERWALK (BOTH SIDES OF RIVER)
6. THEATER DISTRICT
7. NEW HOUSING #1
8. BREWERY DISTRICT
9. NEW HOUSING #2
10. PLAZA EAST OFFICE CENTER
11. NORTHWESTERN MUTUAL LIFE PARKING STRUCTURE
12. NORTHWESTERN MUTUAL LIFE PLACE
13. 411 E. WISCONSIN BUILDING
14. WAREHOUSE DISTRICT

31. *Downtown Milwaukee, showing the Grand Avenue and the location of other developments that it has influenced.*

earth to make it happen. Public officials and corporate leaders worked long hours to make The Grand Avenue the best it could be with the threat of failure looming over their labors. People put their careers on the line to support a project that conventional wisdom said first couldn't happen, and second would be a flop if it did happen." [4]

From the point of view of catalytic urban design, the success of the Grand Avenue goes far beyond the bold vision, money, and political muscle that brought it into being. The value of the Grand Avenue is only partly itself; it is equally valuable for its subsequent effects, the way it was able to catalyze other development. The section that follows analyzes this catalysis.

1. THE NEW ELEMENT MODIFIES THE ELEMENTS AROUND IT

Hyatt Hotel and Federal Plaza.   Even before the Grand Avenue was built, it began to have side effects. Agreements to erect a new hotel and a federal office building nearby were obtained from third parties, along with support for these efforts from the city. Thus the catalyst begins to structure a receptive environment even before it takes physical shape. Although it might appear that the hotel and federal building caused the Grand Avenue, the opposite is closer to the truth.

Skywalk System.   One of the early by-products of this interaction between the Grand Avenue, the Federal Building, and the Hyatt Hotel was a skywalk system, a second-level pedestrian network to link these elements with an existing convention center and, ultimately, other parts of downtown. The system has already been extended east across the Milwaukee River, and further extensions are planned: west to the Marc Plaza Hotel and possibly east beyond the Marine Bank Building.

East Town.   Some critics of the Grand Avenue development had predicted that the area east of the Milwaukee River, called East Town, would suffer from the new commercial attraction to the west. A view of the world that assumes a finite number of shoppers with a finite amount of disposable income would have to draw such a conclusion. But catalysts, while recognizing and respecting natural limits, can unleash and coalesce energy and attract interest that is not otherwise apparent in the field. For example, the Grand Avenue has attracted custom from broader realms. Whereas downtown had been deserted on weekends, suddenly it was attracting sixty thousand people during those two days, and twenty to twenty-five thousand every weekday.[5] So instead of robbing East Town of custom, it has brought more shoppers. East Town merchants acknowledge that there has been a spillover effect; their East Town Association reported "constant sales increases month after month" after the Grand Avenue opened.[6]

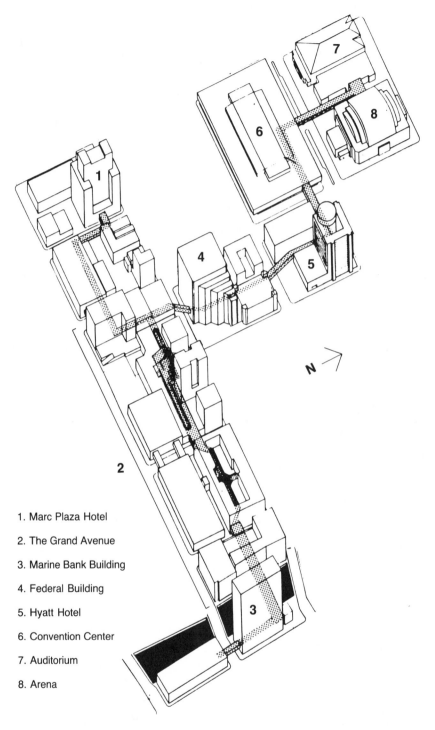

1. Marc Plaza Hotel

2. The Grand Avenue

3. Marine Bank Building

4. Federal Building

5. Hyatt Hotel

6. Convention Center

7. Auditorium

8. Arena

32. The emerging skywalk system. All except the extension to the Marc Plaza Hotel has been built.

Riverwalk. Bridging the Milwaukee River with a skywalk to East Town not only made a symbolic and practical connection but also gave impetus to a long-standing dream of turning the Milwaukee River into an urban amenity. Earlier, incidental, efforts to address the possibilities of the river now could be linked because of a real commitment, a belief in the value and the plausibility of a riverwalk system. Design specifications for it have been written.

Apart from serving as an amenity, a riverwalk will bridge a conceptual gap between commercial Milwaukee, as represented by Wisconsin Avenue businesses, and cultural Milwaukee, represented by the Performing Arts Center on the river several blocks to the north. A riverwalk system will link these and, more important, will provide support for another by-product of downtown rejuvenation: a theater district.

Theater District. For several years the Milwaukee Repertory Theater had been searching for a space of its own, designed for its needs. Among its options was an unused power plant on the river halfway between Wisconsin Avenue and the Performing Arts Center. The lively new configuration of downtown represented in the Grand Avenue not only made the power plant location reasonable but also unleashed a slightly grander vision of a theater complex and activity node that would be a focus for the offerings of the Milwaukee Repertory Theater as well as those of the adjacent historic Pabst Theater and Performing Arts Center. The Grand Avenue thus gave the shot of confidence needed to spur investment in a mixed-use development associated with the theater district.[7] The focus of the new theater district is an arcadelike space supported economically by residential, office, and retail uses. Called Milwaukee Center, this node is conceived as a way of increasing and enhancing nightlife downtown, thus strengthening and supporting the Grand Avenue's shopping and service activities.

Extension of the Grand Avenue. The effects of the Grand Avenue are also being felt to the west. The Grand Avenue is expected to generate its own extension by enveloping an additional city block and by making an important skywalk connection to the Marc Plaza Hotel (shown in Figure 32).

West of Downtown. Further west, interest has been kindled in improving the connection between downtown and the area around Marquette University, now separated by the expressway. Discussions have been held and plans proposed to bridge this gulf. The Grand Avenue has proved that downtown can be attractive, thus giving impetus and reassurance to those who wish to upgrade this transitional area to the west.

Warehouse District. Even before the completion of the Grand Avenue, an area of underutilized loft buildings, warehouses, and produce markets to the south had been talked about as an asset to the city. Cer-

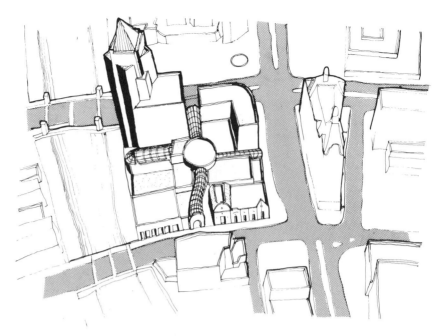

33. Proposed Milwaukee Center, part of the new theater district (City Hall to the right, Performing Arts Center above).

tainly, similar areas in other cities have been transformed and made economically viable. But until the Grand Avenue catalyzed a new "can-do" attitude, no real progress was made. The Third Ward warehouse district is now, however, experiencing a renaissance.

New Housing.   Further afield, the impact of the Grand Avenue and related developments has inspired confidence that housing downtown will be desired if downtown itself is desirable. A townhouse development on the river has appeared, and land belonging to the Juneau Village urban renewal project that had remained vacant since the 1960s has become the site of middle- and upper-income housing. Called Yankee Hill, this project is a joint venture of the Milwaukee Redevelopment Corporation and a private developer, Madsen, the first to follow the Grand Avenue.

Brewery District.   North of downtown, plans are under way to adapt for reuse two former breweries, one of which had been lying idle for years. An earlier concept for its adaptive reuse (Figure 123) was revised and implemented.

Although one way of characterizing the catalytic process in Milwaukee is to identify the physical increments of revitalization and transformation, the developments themselves, it is equally important to recognize the transformation in attitude that the Grand Avenue has engendered:

34. New housing along the east bank of the Milwaukee River, designed by William Wenzler Associates, architects (City Hall in background).

35. Yankee Hill housing. Forty-four townhouses and two housing towers, designed by Kahler Slater Tophy Engberg, architects. This joint venture by the Madsen Corporation and the Milwaukee Redevelopment Corporation followed the MRC's success with the Grand Avenue.

36. *Cartoon by Brian Duffy celebrating the Grand Avenue, published in* Milwaukee Magazine, *November 1982.*

I can't say that nothing would have happened downtown if the Grand Avenue hadn't happened—that's not true. But I don't know if people would have been as bullish about the redevelopment potential of the central city. I can tell you that the attitude in Milwaukee has changed from "The downtown is dead" to "Anything is possible and we can probably make it happen."[8]

According to John Wellhoefer, Dragos's successor at the MRC, "the success of the Grand Avenue meant a complete 180-degree turn in the sentiment about investing in Downtown Milwaukee. It used to be okay to work Downtown. Now it's a place people want to go to see and be seen."[9]

For Edmund Bacon, commenting on the transformation of downtown Milwaukee, "The real driving force of making a city become vibrant, alive and economically feasible rests in establishing in the collective mind of the people what the city can become."[10] The Grand Avenue and the chain reaction it has unleashed have created a situation in which "people want a renaissance of downtown to happen. . . . Today the general opinion is that downtown redevelopment should continue bigger and better, and that virtually anything is possible if we put our collective minds to it."[11]

All of the visions that accompany this flush of civic enthusiasm cannot be accommodated. Not everything can happen. What is important is that suddenly some dreams that had been thought unrealistic seem possible.

2. EXISTING ELEMENTS ARE ENHANCED OR TRANSFORMED IN POSITIVE WAYS

This principle is manifested in two ways, in buildings and in people's behavior. In the case of the Grand Avenue, the Plankinton Arcade, which had withered in both its role and its physical condition, was refurbished and given a new life as the centerpiece of the Grand Avenue development. Previously remote from the action of Wisconsin Avenue, the arcade is now the skylit crossroads of the complex. Behavioral patterns have changed, too. Downtown in Milwaukee traditionally had meant retailing, but the range of retail activity had declined with the appearance of suburban shopping centers. In less than two years following the development of the Grand Avenue, downtown was once again the prime center in the Milwaukee retail market.

37. Original design drawing for the long interior space of the Plankinton Arcade. Holabird and Roche, architects, 1916.

Restoration and preservation need no justification; their utility and economic sense are proven. It is instructive, however, to identify the range of attitudes that characterized even this one revitalization project.

Restoration.   The Plankinton Arcade had an architectural character and a physical organization that suited the concept for the Grand Avenue; in fact, with its interior circulation spine, it established the pattern for the whole complex. The arcade had been unsympathetically modified; it needed only to be restored.

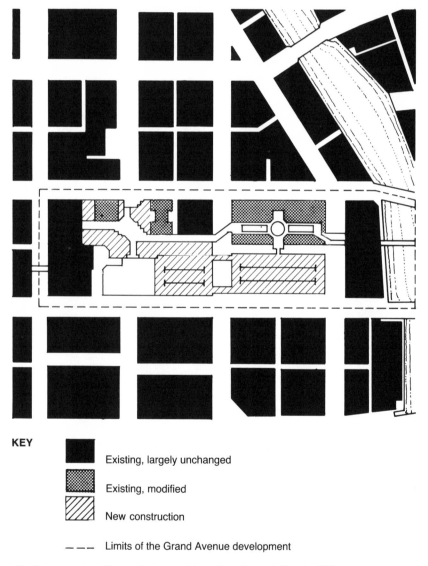

KEY

▮ Existing, largely unchanged

▨ Existing, modified

▱ New construction

— — — Limits of the Grand Avenue development

38. New construction respects and incorporates existing buildings.

Modification.   Buildings in the block west of the Plankinton Arcade had a conventional orientation to the street and turned their backs to the service alley to the rear. Here the task was to give these buildings a dual orientation without compromising their architectural character or functional utility. The Woolworth Building required the most extensive changes. The two existing department stores needed only to add interior aisles to connect with the skywalks.

It would be misleading to suggest that nothing is destroyed in a catalytic process. At the Grand Avenue, the old (but unexceptional) Plankinton Hotel had to make way for a needed parking structure. Other, minor, commercial and office structures were also destroyed. But landmark buildings like Gimbels (now Marshall Field), the Plankinton Arcade, and Boston Store remained. The commercial flavor of Wisconsin Avenue was retained. The key to enhancing and transforming rather than destroying the context is to formulate a plan that retains and improves places characterized by good architectural and urban design; often such a plan requires a patchwork approach to development, one that incorporates existing buildings instead of cleaning the urban slate.

Sometimes social costs are associated with large developments like the Grand Avenue, but this was not the case in Milwaukee, since there was little housing in the area being developed. And, if anything, the improvements seem to have created jobs.

3. THE CATALYTIC REACTION DOES NOT DAMAGE ITS CONTEXT

Milwaukee's Wisconsin Avenue was a typical linear shopping street with surprisingly little retailing depth, in most cases no more than half a block. This configuration required long walks between shops, often in bad weather. To compete with the comfort and compact form of suburban shopping malls, shopping in a revitalized downtown would need to be consolidated and shoppers sheltered, without spurning the rest of downtown in the process.

The configuration of the Grand Avenue achieves these aims by opening many ground-floor shops to both the street and the interior concourse. Thus the Grand Avenue creates a focus adjacent to Wisconsin Avenue without destroying the traditional character of the avenue in the process.

Although they are not a characteristic of all urban catalysts, the benign edges of the Grand Avenue moderate its impact on its context. Its end points, Boston Store and Marshall Field, and most of its frontage on Wisconsin Avenue remain as they were before. The project does not extensively inject new forms; it does not dramatically disrupt downtown's established architectural character. Instead, the Grand Avenue adds space and form *within* the existing pattern of the city. It is noteworthy that a radical reorganization of pedestrian space could be accomplished without radically affecting the architectural character of downtown.

39. The context of the Grand Avenue before construction (looking west).

40. The context of the Grand Avenue after construction (looking east). The new Grand Avenue entrance—the only new frontage on Wisconsin Avenue—occupies a section of North Third Street (east of the Woolworth store).

Admittedly, many revitalization projects do not begin with buildings in place that remain useful and have strong architectural character—like the Plankinton Arcade and the Marshall Field store. In those projects it is not possible to leave what exists as benign edges. Nevertheless, whatever edges remain can still have an important impact, for a building or a development offers cues to what could or should follow from it on adjacent sites. Existing parking structures along Michigan Avenue, one block south, seemed to suggest that street as a site for the Grand Avenue's parking needs. Creating a major pedestrian entrance where Third Street was closed suggested a public space node there—and the design of the Federal Building responded by creating Federal Plaza. Skywalks connecting segments of the Grand Avenue suggested skywalks to extend the web of connections beyond the shopping complex. Such design cues are an important part of the catalytic process.

The responsibility for containing side effects lies not with the architects of development A but with the developers, owners, architects, and municipal overseers of subsequent developments B, C, D, and so forth. Although there is an inclination to capitalize on increased land values created by a catalyst, it is important to use the new resource imaginatively and with restraint. An excellent example of such imaginative restraint is the refurbishment of the Iron Block building a block from the Grand Avenue. The city's only remaining commercial building with a cast-iron facade, it had been left to decline. Given its corner location on Wisconsin Avenue and its proximity to the new catalyst, the Iron Block site might have been exploited. But instead a thoughtful reclamation has taken place—evidence of laudable restraint that improves the quality of downtown without sacrificing an owner's opportunity to profit from the turn of events.

4. A POSITIVE CATALYTIC REACTION REQUIRES AN UNDERSTANDING OF THE CONTEXT

Architectural and Urban Character. There is a tendency to think of retail design in relation to suburban precedents; urban architecture, however, should be more sensitive than this. The revitalization of downtown requires architecture appropriate to the downtown, not contrived atmosphere or generic design. "There's no rationale behind a suburban transplant in the central city," says Stephen Dragos. "It won't work." To compete successfully and attract additional investment, a downtown center "has to be something that uplifts the spirit, that's superior to everything else in the surrounding area. That was our objective, so we had to get the best."[12]

The architecture of the historical center city can be differentiated from that of the suburbs through historicizing motifs. But too often these motifs are no more than pastiche. A more sympathetic response to historical architecture can be achieved by understanding its *principles*. For example, in the Grand Avenue the shape of the cross section is tighter

41. Iron Block, built in 1860 (refurbished in 1984). George H. Johnson, architect.

42. Interior of the Plankinton Arcade, whose refurbishment was part of the Grand Avenue development. Refurbishment architects: ELS / Elbasani and Logan, 1983.

43. Arcade in a new portion of the Grand Avenue. ELS / Elbasani and Logan, architects, 1983.

and more vertical—more intensive and classically urban—than that of suburban malls.

Other elements, in concert with this intense vertical cross section, contribute to a sense of urbanity: the colonnade at the edge of the balcony lends a sense of intimacy different from the vacuousness of typical mall spaces. The pitched skylights are reminiscent of nineteenth-century skylights and give a strong sense of daylighted interior space. More specific period references are found at a smaller scale: sconces and Tivoli lights, for example.

In relation to this concern for responding to the existing architectural and urban character of downtown, the most questionable decision at the Grand Avenue was the closing of Third Street. Did this disrupt traffic in and violate the perceptions of downtown? There is no evidence that the street closure has impeded the flow of traffic, and the closure does not hamper the movement of pedestrians. In fact, it invites pedestrians, for this is the principal entrance to the Grand Avenue. Although this modification in street pattern seems not to have been excessive, violations of the character of an existing setting remain a concern in any project that begins to restructure downtown in dramatic ways.

Composition of People and Ingredients.   Whereas homogeneity is a feature of suburban malls, downtowns are distinctively heterogeneous. Thus strong efforts were made to secure tenants for the Grand Avenue to mirror the character of Milwaukee and Milwaukeeans. In fact, "Rouse actively recruited local merchants for the center in order to give the Grand Avenue a distinctly Milwaukee flavor."[13] When the Grand Avenue opened, 48 percent of the tenants were local merchants, 12 percent regional, and 40 percent national.[14]

Although there is a legitimate criticism of gentrification when it overwhelms neighborhoods and eliminates housing for low-income people, the gentrification of downtown Milwaukee has not been exploitative but represents good planning. Historical precedent suggests that a healthy downtown is one with a mix of people, shops, and activities; in too many American cities it has become the sole province of the poor. To rebuild downtown Milwaukee and make it a center for everyone again meant understanding the values of and giving certain assurances to the middle-class shoppers on whom most strong commercial areas—and certainly downtowns—depend.

Image.   The Grand Avenue had to reverse the image of downtown as unsafe, the home of undesirables. It overcame this considerable psychological barrier by reintroducing stores attractive to middle-class buyers, by locating parking close to shopping, and by insisting on a high standard of design. Further, the Grand Avenue is marketed not as competition for suburban malls but as something special: "It's an experience to be here as much as it is to shop here. . . . Extra touches lend an air of spontaneity, a festival feeling that you don't always find at suburban malls," says Paula Boyd, the advertising and marketing manager.[15] It is remarkable that in Milwaukee this transformation in image was accomplished in a matter of months: "The history of The Grand Avenue proves that downtown in its bloom could be a powerful magnet to attract the suburban and urban shopper. We proved that downtown's image could be changed virtually overnight."[16] Especially remarkable, the image of downtown was transformed largely through this single development.

Parking.   To compete with suburban shopping centers, the Grand Avenue had to provide even more convenient parking at an affordable price. Covered parking for 1,350 cars adjacent to the Grand Avenue assures shoppers of a short, well-lighted walk protected from inclement weather. As a result, according to a Boston Store representative, customers feel safer here than they do in suburban malls.[17] The cost of parking has been adjusted to encourage short-term shopping and to discourage long-term use by office workers or people with time-consuming business outside the Grand Avenue.

5. ALL CATALYTIC REACTIONS ARE NOT THE SAME

The chemistry for urban revitalization in Milwaukee depended on several elements, first among them the configuration of traffic and traditional uses of the setting. For example, the linear character of the Wisconsin Avenue commercial district is unlike that of cities whose shopping activities have developed around an intersection or a square. And because of land costs, access from freeways, and other considerations, parking tends to be concentrated.

Second, such unique ingredients as the Plankinton Arcade and service alleys parallel to Wisconsin Avenue give the Grand Avenue a configuration different from one in which stores fill whole blocks or where there is no inviting interior semipublic space. Further, the two existing department stores two blocks apart on the same side of Wisconsin Avenue argued for the linear character of the Grand Avenue. In a city with another set of existing elements, a different configuration for development would have emerged.

Third, socio-political and economic conditions were instrumental in facilitating changes. The individuals associated with the Milwaukee Redevelopment Corporation and those in city government helped both to make the Grand Avenue seem feasible and to implement it. The development of the Grand Avenue depended upon agreements to begin certain other developments, like the Hyatt Hotel and the new Federal Building. Then, too, the development probably would not have gone ahead with-

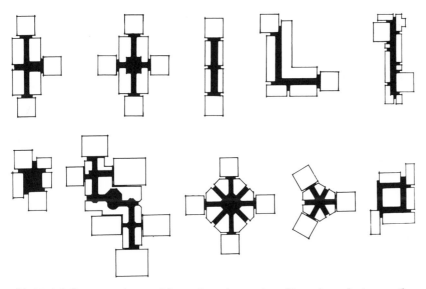

44. Nodal, linear, and spread-form shopping centers. Stores in a cluster are the equivalent of shops around a square; stretched out, they are like shops along Main Street. Either of these configurations can be extended to create spread-form variations.

out tax-increment financing, which gave useful leverage: "We're taking something that doesn't exist to begin with and leveraging it to accomplish something else." [18]

In summary, center city developments must be conceived as unique collections of existing ingredients needing to be customized to satisfy new sets of requirements. Center city development calls for both idealism and pragmatism: idealism about the specialness of the place and pragmatism about making that place work in relation to contemporary traffic needs and local culture and values. This dual need calls for nothing short of a unique vision for each such urban place.

6. CATALYTIC DESIGN IS STRATEGIC

Although much urban development is opportunistic ("Take advantage of tax credits; buy when prices are low; build what's profitable wherever you can"), better guarantees of profitability and urban quality can be had from strategic rather than opportunistic thinking. Opportunists think of the short term; strategists, of the longer term.

Goals.   Catalytic urban design is based on formulas and programs, not specific plans and designs. It works not from a master plan, but from a master program. The distinction is now familiar to urban planners but is still worth repeating. Whereas a master plan specifies an end condition in the future, a master program sets more general objectives and identifies ways of achieving them. In effect, a program offers several ways to reach the objective—depending on circumstances. And it sets out intentions and methods but not solutions.

So, for example, a classic master plan establishes transportation, zoning, and land use patterns years or even decades hence and is typically inflexible in responding to changing circumstances; a master program sets out to stimulate and control development in a way more responsive to the exigencies and opportunities that appear in potentially volatile American cities. In short, a master program is flexible. The key to keeping strategic and catalytic design malleable is to have multiple rather than single-minded views of the future.

Zoning as Control, Guide, and Incentive.   Stephen Dragos advised those concerned with the quality of Milwaukee's revitalization to be cautious. "Developers will jump at the chance to build near a Rouse project [like the Grand Avenue]. But Milwaukee must resist the temptation to jump at the first offer that comes along. . . . We have to ask: What do we expect? What do we want to happen?" [19]

New zoning restrictions for downtown Milwaukee are intended to direct the impact of new development strategically. Use districts have been identified: shopping, corporate headquarters, housing, government services, culture, and entertainment. Areas are designated, each with its own characteristics: shops and retail stores around the Grand Avenue; taller buildings along the east bank of the river, lower buildings facing west from East Town; Kilbourn Avenue a "showcase boulevard," with hotels and other buildings along tree-lined walks; the brewery district near the Performing Arts Center a mix of shops, restaurants, and housing that has been converted from commercial buildings; warehouses and factories ringing downtown; housing in most of the districts. The new zoning plan assumes that riverwalks will be developed.

In addition to flexible land use considerations, design guidelines or development controls should be part of a city's strategy for shaping itself. Planners need to influence visual as well as land use design.

Sequencing Development.   In the sequencing of development, as much as anywhere, the distinction between master programs and master plans is evident. Each step of a master program determines and depends upon previous stages and real events, not a scheme for a distant future. What happens and when is far more important than an image of an end product. For example, it would have been pointless to specify the Grand Avenue without predicating the Hyatt Hotel and Federal Building that made it feasible. Similarly, without the Grand Avenue and other connections, the skywalk system would make no sense; in its turn it made a riverwalk development logical. The riverwalk can eventually tie in to a theater district. And so forth.

Although such sequencing is a key characteristic of catalytic design, in fact in the urban setting events are seldom that controllable. It is probably more accurate to think of strategic design as a web of opportunities that are created and seized upon rather than as a linear development.

7. A PRODUCT BETTER THAN THE SUM OF
THE INGREDIENTS

In Milwaukee the auditorium / convention center was an island. Now it is tied tightly to the Hyatt Hotel and to downtown by the skywalk system. The connections are practical, but the conceptual linkage of the disparate parts may be more important than practicality. The goal of any catalytic reaction should be not a collection of developments—so often the case in revitalization schemes—but *integrative urbanism* in which the parts reinforce one another and each is better for its association with the others.

Integrative Urban Architecture.   Individually, few buildings in downtown Milwaukee are exceptional architecturally. But collectively they make a unique place. Marshall Field, Boston Store, Woolworth's, and the Plankinton Arcade had been separate entities. Now each is improved and more profitable because it has been *related* to the others in a meaningful way.

Relating these buildings has created large semipublic interior spaces where only one, the Plankinton Arcade, had existed before. In the process, a new kind of architecture has been added to the city—yet it is not alien but has physical and visual precedents. The industrial aesthetic of the Grand Avenue design integrates turn-of-the-century glazed metal-frame systems and contemporary high-tech images.

Ongoing Catalysis.   Careful redevelopment can mean economic development, which fosters further redevelopment: "The dream was to turn a somewhat dormant Downtown Milwaukee, into an alive and vibrant, moving showplace. The Grand Avenue does that. But it can do more. It can serve as the catalyst for other economic development in the Downtown area. It can be the source for hundreds of new jobs." [20] The vitality of a catalytic reaction has far greater potential than the visionless, haphazard process of opportunistic development.

Building Confidence.   When citizens get more than they expected from public investment, when the very image of their city is recast through thoughtful design and strategic planning, they will give more and take part more eagerly. Even as the Grand Avenue was setting economic records and turning doubters into enthusiasts, critics wondered whether it would be a catalyst that sets off other actions or a development so large that it saps the community's resources. Critics also suggested waiting to see. But Dragos and others advised a different course: this was just the beginning. It was "not a time to pull back and say, 'Well, let's wait five years to see if this works or not.' What will make it work best is to take the next steps." [21] The wealth of projects precipitated by the Grand Avenue suggests that Milwaukee did not wait.

8. THE CATALYST CAN REMAIN IDENTIFIABLE

In chemistry the catalyst often disappears or is transformed in the course of a reaction, but this is usually not the case with urban chemistry. Instead, the ingredients of rejuvenation remain and contribute to the city's unique character and sense of depth. The layers of urban experience and urban history, the collage of styles and uses characteristic of a vital center city are the essence of urbanity. In fact, one of the pleasures of the center city is to trace and reconstruct the events that have produced its distinctive character: bold street grids; riverside industry; Main Street commercialism; technological bravado in iron, steel, and concrete; proud civic structures; and so forth. Total renewal and total design are largely discredited. A collage of overlaid urban visions and of identifiably different parts, an overlapping, sedimentary record of various decades and their architects, is much preferred. Cities are richer for the variety.

From the point of view of architects, that their contributions to the city are recognizable is good for business; at the same time they get credit for weaving in rather than imposing their own personal visions. In Milwaukee, the Grand Avenue intertwines with what has come before, amending and revising but not overwhelming.

45. Sedimentation, accretion, and layering of urban form in Milwaukee.

It is taking the dedication of many individuals and organizations to re-generate Milwaukee. Institutional, civic, and political action set the process in motion and made possible the key factor, the Grand Avenue. Although the economics and politics involved in the catalytic process are of unquestioned importance, the focus of this analysis is catalysts as a tool in urban design. Just as investment begets investment, so too does (or should) good design beget good design. Buildings *do* set precedents, and these matter. The Grand Avenue is thoughtfully conceived and sensitively designed, and it has the potential to inspire other development, to improve the character and the quality of subsequent work, and to link up with existing and new construction.

To understand the importance of the catalytic concept in urban and architectural design, consider what might have happened had the Grand Avenue been different, had it been conceived and built as a suburban shopping center transposed to downtown. Would it have evoked the pride suggested in Brian Duffy's cartoon (Figure 36)? Would suburbanites have been induced to change shopping patterns and drive downtown instead of to the nearest mall? Would the Grand Avenue have restructured the rankings of commercial centers in the region?

There is a danger in urban development not only of failing to have an impact but of actually inhibiting new development through inadvisable actions. A negative catalyst is as much a possibility as a positive one. A development can act like a sponge in soaking up resources and activity, depriving adjacent areas. It can fail to inspire responses. Failure to light a spark can discourage others from investing time, effort, and financial resources. Programs, strategies, and designs need to be properly conceived if dynamic, productive catalysis is to happen.

We contend both that urban catalysis was necessary to accomplish what has been accomplished in downtown Milwaukee and what is continuing to happen there and that unilateral, univalent renewal could not have met the challenge. The accomplishment is considerable:

- A unique *place* is emerging, a place composed of and responsive to what was there before. It is both old and new.

- It is for many a new *gateway* to a city they had abandoned, thus helping to restructure the image of downtown.

- It *establishes precedents* for other developments—precedents in design quality, precedents for thinking about existing buildings, precedents for using the city, precedents for relating interior-oriented architecture to existing streets and street life, and precedents for an integrative urban architecture that is new in the experience of most Milwaukeeans.

Master plans could not have accomplished what has happened in Milwaukee and what continues to happen there; nor could functionalist,

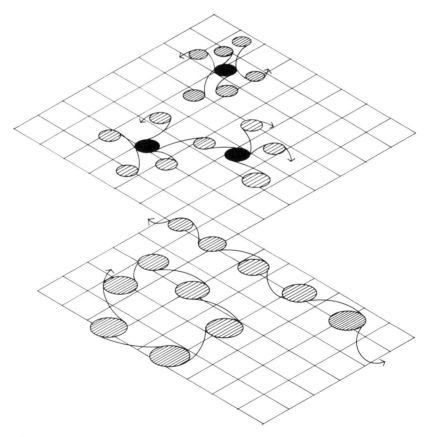

46. *Catalytic reactions can take several forms: nuclear (top), multi-nucleated, serial, and "necklace" (lower left).*

structuralist, humanist, or formalist urban design concepts; nor could a raw pragmatic approach. To understand events in Milwaukee as well as in other American cities requires a concept like urban catalysis.

A discussion of the chemistry of urban architecture would be incomplete without reference to the people who make it happen. The urban chemist does not stand outside the process but is integral to and influenced by it. As Milwaukee demonstrates, effective people are as important to the catalytic process as a well-conceived, appropriately staged development. People get the process going.[22] In one city a corporation executive might be instrumental, in other cities a development corporation, a highly respected individual, a popular mayor, or an alliance of citizens.

The context in which urban design strategists work is less predictable than that of laboratory chemists. A collection of ingredients used according to a proven formula will not always yield a particular product or have a reliable consequence. The predictability of the laboratory setting decreases when the lab is a city. This is not to say that urban chemistry is entirely indeterminate and unpredictable, only that it is less predictable than chemistry in the laboratory and that it is subject to subtle influences. The catalytic process does not necessarily move methodically from step A through steps B, C, and D but might bounce around in a looser (though not random) fashion before achieving a desired end. The architect and urban designer Robert M. Beckley has related this semideterminate process to that of a pinball machine. The catalyst is unleashed within a limited field, but its precise path and its accomplishments are determined in part by inexorable forces (like gravity), skill with flippers, nudges, and accident. The human ingredient of urban catalysis is evident in efforts to set the process in motion; in considered use of flippers (knowledge, money, IOUs); and nudging at the right time and with appropriate finesse. In an indeterminate context, "chemists" are needed to keep the process going.

To elaborate further the concept of urban catalysis and to demonstrate that the process works in other cities and in cities of varying size, we examine a number of other cases in the next chapter.

4

CATALYSTS IN ACTION

Although Milwaukee provides an especially clear example of the potential of catalytic urban design, the principle is demonstrated in other cities as well. It is noteworthy that the size of a city is not a condition; small cities as well as large can undergo and benefit from catalytic transformation.

KALAMAZOO: THE NEW ELEMENT MODIFIES THE ELEMENTS AROUND IT

In Milwaukee the Grand Avenue inspired and supported subsequent developments, including the riverwalk system, skywalk system, theater district, and the Third Ward historic district revitalization. These events in turn gave impetus to new housing, the revival of the brewery district idea, and so forth. In Kalamazoo, Michigan, a similar series of events and consequences may be seen.[1] Kalamazoo is a midsize regional center with a population of approximately 100,000. The Upjohn Company (pharmaceuticals) is a major force in the community. As in many other small cities, in the 1950s and 1960s the retail center in Kalamazoo was challenged by suburban shopping centers. The first response seems to have been to imitate suburban complexes. When that approach failed, other tacks were taken, not always successfully. The key to Kalamazoo's achievement is a collection of efforts that support one another. Several mileposts mark the city's efforts to regenerate its core over a period of years through a catalytic chain reaction.

Antedating the redevelopment efforts of Kalamazoo was a key 1957–1958 study by Victor Gruen Associates. It identified the causes of center city decline and recommended a radical restructuring of the city's core. Like systemic/functionalist schemes of the same period, the Gruen recommendation called for an efficient one-way traffic loop around downtown, tied to vast parking areas ringing a pedestrianized commercial precinct. Conceptually, downtown Kalamazoo would be an urban, rather than suburban, shopping center. Gruen's scheme for a 180-acre area in Kalamazoo may be compared to the 164-acre development for Detroit's Northland shopping center, which Gruen designed at about the same time.

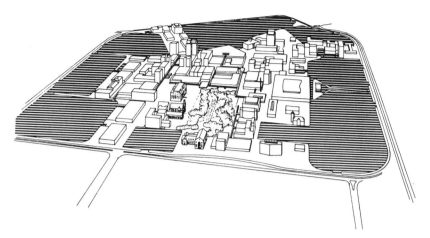

47. *Kalamazoo as it might appear if developed like a shopping center. Shaded areas represent peripheral parking.*

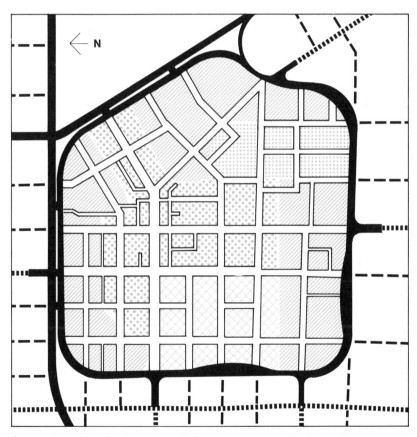

48. *Land use plan for downtown Kalamazoo suggested by Victor Gruen Associates. The central dotted area would be commercial; areas to the west and east would be, respectively, civic and cultural, and research and hospital. Parking for cars would be on the periphery.*

Gruen's recommendations were beyond the capabilities of a town of eighty-five thousand. The purchase and clearing of land for parking lots, the transformation of city streets into pleasant malls, and the construction of a circumferential roadway would cost too much, even if they were politically feasible, which they probably were not. The Gruen plan gave Kalamazoo an impossible, unbuildable vision of the future.

Although studies like Gruen's can have positive effects, arousing public interest and changing perceptions, they can also be dangerous. Because total redevelopment is seldom economically feasible, piecemeal redevelopment is sometimes attempted. But in a scheme like Gruen's each part depends upon the others; it is unlikely that any one element can succeed on its own. Isolated restructurings, left uncoordinated, can devastate and rend a city. Furthermore, impossible visions can engender cynicism; people who recognize that the vision proposed is impossible conclude that nothing can be done.

In Kalamazoo the Gruen vision was not rejected, nor was it built. Instead it prepared an attitudinal base from which more modest and appropriate urban design action could grow. Grandiose visions like Gruen's that arouse interest and change attitudes should not be built; it takes more than an efficient (functionalist/systemic) traffic scheme to revitalize and reaffirm a city center.

Kalamazoo Mall (1959). The first reaction to the stimulus of Gruen's plan was a three-part program:

1. To recast the congested main shopping street as the first permanent (if modest) pedestrian mall in the United States. This change was accompanied by facelifts of and improvements to the stores and office buildings along the new mall.

2. To streamline the downtown traffic system. Instead of constructing a new high-speed ring road, the city converted existing streets to one-way, multi-laned arterials.

3. To form a nonprofit development corporation empowered to buy, sell, and manage property, especially near the mall. It is worth noting that Gruen disapproved of this approach. From his point of view, the pedestrian mall could succeed only when the traffic problem was solved in a comprehensive and up-to-date way:

> The creation of pedestrian areas downtown can be successful only if it is accomplished as an integral part of an overall plan. In fact it is probably one of the last measures for implementation within a carefully scheduled revitalization plan, and it just cannot be the beginning. Only after proper access from suburban areas toward the central business district has been achieved for private as well as public transportation, only after a belt road system around the downtown core together with directly adjoining terminal facilities for public transportation and storage facilities for private cars has been constructed, only after a system for servicing downtown buildings has been implemented, can the creation of pedestrian districts be accomplished.[2]

Central Parkway South Urban Renewal Project (1963–1967).

If the scope and sequence of revitalization in Kalamazoo did not satisfy Gruen, the community's attitude must have. Kalamazoo did not stop with a modest mall and streamlined traffic system but looked for other action that needed to be taken.

Barton-Aschman Associates recommended changes to an extensive area south of downtown, including the rehabilitation and conservation of one-third of the area's structures; the development of Gruen's ring road through the area; the construction of medium- and high-density housing; the expansion of the pedestrian mall; and increased facilities for offices, light industry, and parking. This scheme, like Gruen's, was too extensive for its political and social setting. It failed to achieve a balance with other ingredients of the community. It failed to acknowledge the realities of its time and place and was rejected in a 1968 referendum for several reasons. First, though some housing was designated for rehabilitation, other housing would have been demolished. This seemed wasteful and unnecessary to the townspeople. Second, the projected ring road appeared to be a barrier to movement between the neighborhood and downtown. Third, the city's subsidy of private development seemed wrong. That the city would purchase private property, level buildings, and resell the land at a lower price seemed un-American in conservative Kalamazoo. Finally, the specter of public housing frightened some voters.[3]

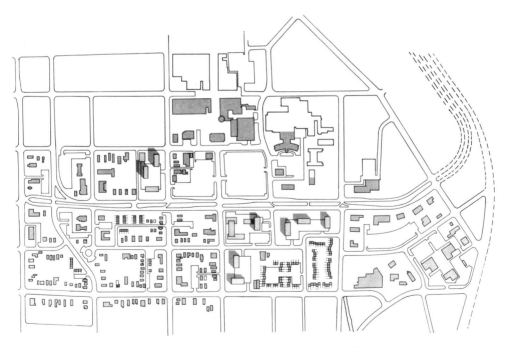

49. *The Barton-Aschman scheme for the area south of downtown Kalamazoo, based on the architects' drawing.*

In summary, the Central Parkway South project was too big for and alien to Kalamazoo in the late 1960s. Instead of growing conceptually from what Kalamazoo was, it was to have been a vast formulaic urban renewal scheme imposed upon the city. It was not part of the catalytic chain reaction begun by other events; it was too far from the mall to be an inevitable next step. Moreover, it became a political issue, so it could be voted down.

Extension and Refurbishment of the Pedestrian Mall (1971).
The success of the pedestrian mall gave impetus to its extension and refurbishment, evidence of both its success and its perceived value as an ingredient of downtown. This kind of improvement is not visionary but evidences sound catalytic action.

Improvements to Bronson Hospital (1972–1981) and the Upjohn Company (1974–1985).
Investments by Bronson Hospital and the Upjohn Company demonstrated local confidence in the city and its downtown. These employment centers in turn contribute pedestrian traffic that supports other developments like Kalamazoo Mall.

Kalamazoo Center and Mall Expansion/Renovation (1975).
Though the Kalamazoo Mall was innovative and successful, by itself it could not spur the revitalization of downtown. It needed enhancement. The technique chosen was to create a "magnet" and a "generator" at the most important intersection downtown, the crossing of Michigan Avenue and Kalamazoo Mall. This would give downtown a visual and experiential focal point and would encourage further development of the mall to the north.

Kalamazoo Center is a mixed-use complex including a high-rise hotel, a shopping and entertainment center, and a convention complex. Mixing activities within the complex was intended to guarantee the use of both the complex and downtown beyond conventional shopping/office hours. A hotel, convention center, shops, parking garage, and restaurants are collected around a soaring space that has been called the city's living room. The critic Suzanne Stephens saw in Kalamazoo Center a linking of "two strongly traditional urban forms: the town square and the market place in their 20th-century manifestations (shopping center and convention center) to create urbanity. . . . Unexpected was the public's appropriation of the mostly privately owned atrium space. Most of the visitors regard it as public turf—much like a street." [4]

Although the hotel, which symbolically marks the center of downtown, is the focus of Kalamazoo Center, it does not dominate the intersection. Set back at a diagonal, the hotel creates an edge for the public realm, not a center. Diagonal approaches and setback corners are visual cues indicating accessibility, suggesting that the building is not conventionally self-contained and pulling pedestrians to it.

At the time the complex was conceived, the legality of certain public-private ventures was questioned. The city wanted a civic center; Inland

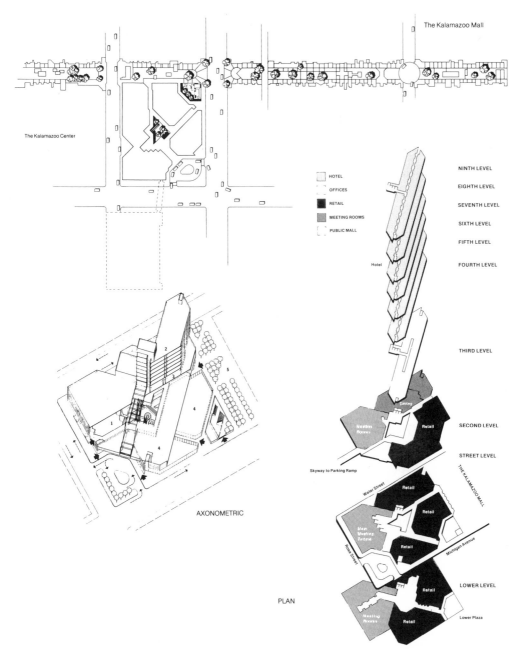

The Kalamazoo Mall

The Kalamazoo Center

HOTEL
OFFICES
RETAIL
MEETING ROOMS
PUBLIC MALL

NINTH LEVEL
EIGHTH LEVEL
SEVENTH LEVEL
SIXTH LEVEL
FIFTH LEVEL
FOURTH LEVEL

THIRD LEVEL

SECOND LEVEL

STREET LEVEL

LOWER LEVEL

Hotel

Dining

Meeting Rooms

Retail

Skyway to Parking Ramp

Water Street

Retail

Retail

Main Meeting Rooms

Retail

Rose Street

Michigan Avenue

THE KALAMAZOO MALL

Retail

Meeting Rooms

Retail

Lower Plaza

AXONOMETRIC

PLAN

50. *Kalamazoo Center, ELS / Elbasani and Logan, architects, 1975. The Center, at a key intersection along Kalamazoo Mall, was conceived as the focus and crossroads of a revitalized downtown.*

51. Kalamazoo Center atrium.

Steel Development Corporation wanted to build a mixed-use center. To avoid possible problems, the complex was erected as two separate structures on separately owned parcels of land.

Building Kalamazoo Mall had been a first step, but by itself the mall could not have withstood the competition of suburban shopping centers. Kalamazoo Center enhanced the mall by focusing activity on it.

Haymarket Historic District (1981). A group of commercial and office structures associated with Kalamazoo's nineteenth-century haymarket has undergone renovation and has been adapted for reuse, forming a cohesive historic district. The area is of strategic importance for its location adjacent to the pedestrian mall and for its role in giving character to Michigan Avenue, the principal artery downtown.

Housing: Hinman South Mall (1983), Arcadia Creek (proposed, 1985).   Housing is acknowledged to be a crucial component of downtown renewal in Kalamazoo, but it must be seen as an integral element rather than an isolated one. Successful housing must make gestures toward further development; it must have "hooks" onto which existing and further development may attach. Hinman South Mall offers luxury condominiums and apartments for senior citizens in conjunction

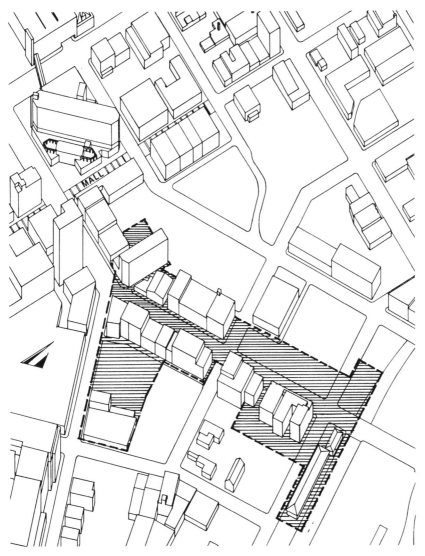

52. *Haymarket Historic District (shaded), Kalamazoo.*

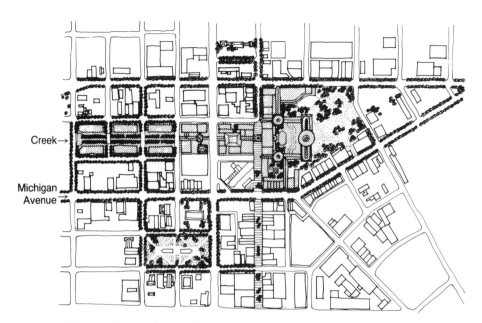

53. Arcadia Creek development, Skidmore Owings and Merrill, architects. Based on the architects' drawings. Housing is conceived as an element of a scheme to renew a declining area on the edge of downtown. An existing creek / drainage ditch would be transformed to create a linear waterside pedestrian spine linking new housing to refurbished loft/office structures and Kalamazoo Mall. Beyond (to the right in the drawing), a conservatory and public garden might be added, too.

with office and commercial space. It appears to be a weak element in the catalytic chain of events, for it is isolated and seems self-contained. It does not acknowledge its context either functionally (when it was built there were few services within walking distance) or architecturally (it makes no effort to recall its context or to guide future development of its neighborhood).

Arcadia Creek seems more promising. An underutilized tract of land near the north end of downtown has been identified for housing development. But instead of quitting at that point, just building housing, the development becomes a vehicle for improving other aspects of downtown. For example, a creek that had been undergrounded through the site will be opened up to become a focal point. Then walkways along the creek will be extended into the existing fabric of downtown—particularly the spaces behind buildings—and will thus transform low-quality residual spaces into positive pedestrian areas.

A related proposal by SOM to transform a vast parking lot into an English garden with a conservatory is more visionary than likely. But this vision alerts us to the possibility that what has been understood as the backsides of Michigan Avenue buildings could become a positive feature

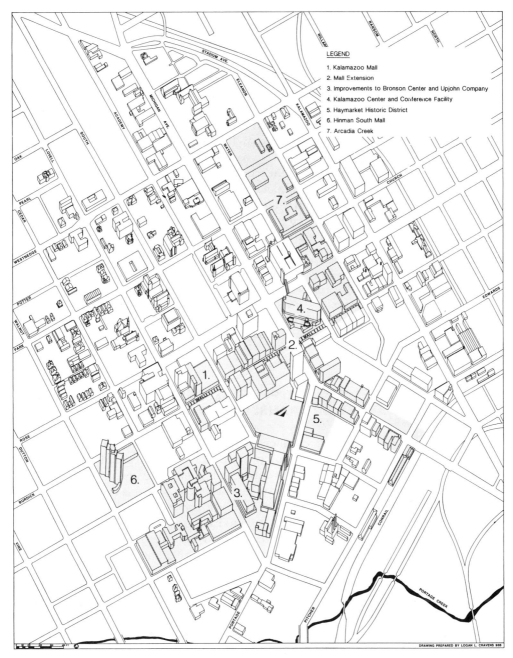

LEGEND

1. Kalamazoo Mall
2. Mall Extension
3. Improvements to Bronson Center and Upjohn Company
4. Kalamazoo Center and Conference Facility
5. Haymarket Historic District
6. Hinman South Mall
7. Arcadia Creek

*54. Kalamazoo since 1957, showing some of the projects undertaken and re-
cently proposed.*

of downtown rather than a residual evil. Informal back elevations can mold and enhance a different kind of urban place. In chapter 5 we characterize this opportunity as a "realm in between."

Although certain elements of Kalamazoo's transformation have been problematic, many have succeeded because they relate to other efforts around them. A proposal to consolidate and redevelop the railroad yards was defeated by voters, but at the same time a twelve-storey office building has appeared across from Kalamazoo Center, and rehabilitations of other buildings downtown have been undertaken. As a whole, events in Kalamazoo support the concept of urban catalysis, in which well-conceived action can impel and support subsequent action.

As important as development projects themselves are vision and leadership like that offered by the Kalamazoo Downtown Development Authority. It calls for a downtown that is

a fascinating, dynamic, unique and pleasant place to work, live and play. Downtown should be more than an eight-hour per day office complex, a noon-hour shopping mall or a part-time center for cultural events. Although it must retain its role as the premier commercial center for the community and Southwestern Michigan, it should also entice us with its liveliness and variety. It should be constantly moving, changing and growing. And, it should be different from every other locale.[5]

SAN ANTONIO AND PHOENIX: EXISTING ELEMENTS ARE ENHANCED OR TRANSFORMED IN POSITIVE WAYS

The Grand Avenue enhanced retailing and employment opportunities in downtown Milwaukee and provided a new architectural setting for the Plankinton Arcade, the Woolworth Building, and several other existing structures. The Kalamazoo pedestrian retail district is reinforced by new developments and renovations nearby. By contrast, numerous shopping mall streets in other cities seem to have speeded up the decline of retail businesses and of employment. Clearly, effective reclamation of existing structures and uses needs strategic, subtle, and well-orchestrated intervention. In a case like Milwaukee's Grand Avenue, where a focus for pedestrian activity was removed from the street, there was a danger that the traditional sense of the existing Main Street along Wisconsin Avenue might be lost, that former fronts of stores might become "backs," that the inward-looking character of shopping centers might turn downtown streets into mere traffic arteries. Although routine development can have such unwanted side effects, thoughtfully conceived catalytic action does not.

The key to saving the pedestrian character of Wisconsin Avenue while introducing an internal pedestrian precinct at midblock was to provide retail space that fronts both on the mall and on the street. This was the pattern in the existing Plankinton Arcade; it was retained and employed elsewhere in the project as well. The existing department stores already stretched through the block; adding midblock circulation increased access. Admittedly, had the census of pedestrians remained constant, the new internal circulation would have reduced pedestrian traffic on city streets. In actuality, the Grand Avenue attracts more people to it, thereby justifying the addition of new pedestrian precincts.

A mixed-use project proposed for downtown Indianapolis similarly demonstrates how a catalyst can enhance existing elements of an area. The program was for retail, office, and hotel uses interwoven with two blocks of existing buildings. Like the Grand Avenue in Milwaukee, the development would be barely noticed from city streets. Circulation and accompanying new construction would occur through the interiors of blocks.

Where new facades are needed, they would be designed in sympathy with existing ones. Although new elements, like a pedestrian bridge and two office towers, are introduced, the overall effect is one of carefully controlled design to protect and strengthen the character of existing buildings.

The case for preserving and recycling existing elements of the urban scene is well established. Ghirardelli Square in San Francisco (1962) provided proof on both aesthetic and economic grounds. Adaptive use is in fact so well established that it is difficult to find a city in which a warehouse or factory has not been reclaimed for another use. Thus it is the

55. Indianapolis: the urban context.

Proposed Circulation Spine

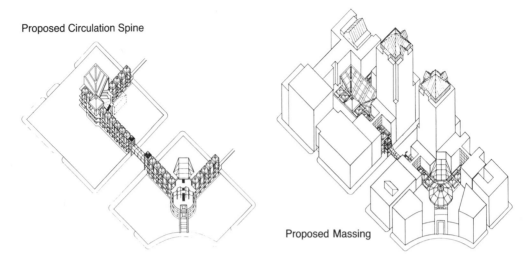

Proposed Massing

56. *Proposed development to be fitted into the Indianapolis context, ELS / Elbasani and Logan, architects.*

catalytic role of adaptations, not adaptive reuse itself, that must be argued, for rehabilitation alone does not ensure new and continuing vitality.

The river in downtown San Antonio, Texas, was not merely reclaimed; it was used as a catalyst to reinvigorate downtown. It is important that the process of rejuvenating riverfront developments did not destroy the very context it was meant to enhance. In some cases, existing buildings addressing the river were merely refurbished. In other instances new developments like the Hyatt and Hilton hotels were pieced into the riverside fabric. At the Hyatt, development created a strong link to the Alamo, thus integrating previously isolated elements of downtown. Larger developments like the convention center and River Center add new elements to the Riverwalk and link the river level to city streets and activities above. River Center, a new shopping complex, ties an existing department store and adjacent city streets to riverside activities. Hence, parts of the city are reclaimed by the intervention of the catalyst. The most common approach, however, was to turn the backs of buildings carefully into riverfronting facades. In most cases this was accomplished while keeping their informal warehouse character.

Finding the value in existing elements of a development like Paseo del Rio is crucial. To recast them would have involved costly artifice. The unique character of the place, so different from that of a commercial downtown, was its central virtue.

In 1985 the city of Phoenix sponsored a competition for the design and planning of a new municipal government complex. Among the objectives were two kinds of effect: to stimulate downtown development and to suggest patterns and attitudes for subsequent design in Phoenix. Many of the competitors approached the problem as though the complex were self-contained. Their dramatic proposals would produce a focal point, an architectural monument, even, that could capture worldwide attention. The new municipal center would upstage the rest of Phoenix.

Other competitors sought to weave the new complex into the city fabric, to make it integral. This meant retaining several of the existing, still usable, structures on the twelve-block site. It meant respecting the reality of downtown Phoenix, which is not a traditional center city commercial district but largely an area of office structures with only limited retail support. It is unrealistic, these competitors argued, to think that shopping patterns can be changed simply through the introduction of shops as part of the new government center. More reasonable is an approach that attaches the new complex to existing services and retail facilities and provides for incremental growth. This approach, instead of surgically implanting an extensive new complex, would graft new facilities incrementally onto existing ones.

Grafting does not mean the uncritical preservation of what exists. Even a modest intervention necessitates some changes in the existing urban

57. *San Antonio. Buildings fronting the river.*

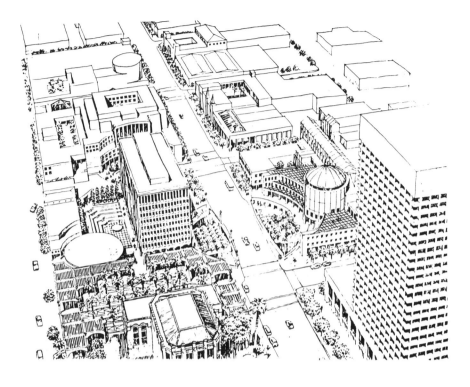

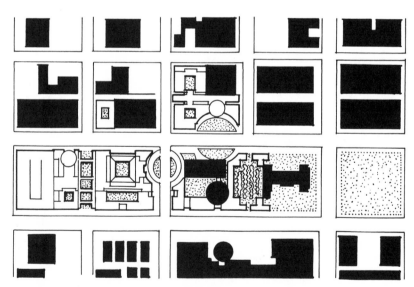

58. "Grafting" of new elements. Competition entry to the Phoenix Municipal Government Center by ELS / Elbasani and Logan and Robert Frankeberger, architects. Instead of upstaging the urban context with an extensive, entirely new complex, this approach recommends gradually attaching new elements to existing ones in a process that evolves a new government center rather than implants it. In the plan (lower part of figure), existing buildings are darkened.

fabric. New and old can mix to produce transformed urban elements. So, for example, competitors proposed that in addition to the historic Dorris Opera House, other buildings in the twelve-block site be refurbished for new use until such time as the city could afford to construct additional government buildings. Instead of planning to clear and build slowly over ten, twenty, or more years, they worked out an incremental strategy to evolve a municipal government center through gradual replacement.

That a catalyst acts moderately, not catastrophically, indicates two values: there is economic value in salvaging existing elements for new uses; and elements with intrinsic urban value continue to enhance the city. It is not necessary to rebuild as though nothing of worth had already been accomplished.

Unfortunately, in an effort to retain the past, historic buildings are too often disfigured and their essential qualities lost. An urban setting can effectively be destroyed even when it is "saved." The practices of patching historical facades as ornaments on much larger buildings and of constructing new buildings to loom over a smaller historical remnant do not

59. Historical facades lose value and significance when treated as an appliqué on much larger new buildings.

transform and enhance the earlier elements but emasculate and carica-ture them. The issue in preservation is not buildings but the spirit of places. A better policy than preservation at any cost, is to seek a new hy-brid of old and new.

GEORGETOWN, WASHINGTON, D.C.: THE CATALYTIC REACTION DOES NOT DAMAGE ITS CONTEXT

In addition to preserving and enhancing elements of value in a project area, urban catalysts treat their contexts with care—in striking contrast both to bulldozer techniques that clear entire areas and to unmoderated changes. Instead, selective demolition and renovation knit new develop-ments into the existing urban fabric. Figure 38 shows how new and reno-vated buildings have been interwoven.

60. Historical character of Georgetown.

61. Canal Square, Georgetown, Arthur Cotton Moore / Associates, architects, 1971. This complex set a standard for subsequent design. It retained the character and scale of street frontages while inserting a respectable modern building within the block. The development makes connections to the C&O canal with a restaurant deck, to historic Georgetown in the selection of materials, and to the pedestrian web with a "town square."

Georgetown was a port that blossomed in the eighteenth and nineteenth centuries. For years it remained a backwater, its residences principally Georgian, its other structures industrial or Victorian. By the twentieth century its waterfront had declined though its residential areas were gradually being reclaimed and refurbished. A Georgetown address began to carry status for residences, though along the Potomac River and Chesapeake & Ohio Railroad canal an industrial slum developed.

Until the early 1970s the few new structures built in Georgetown emulated Colonial styles: brick boxes with regularly spaced double-hung windows, shutters, and occasional ornamental porches. Beginning in the 1970s the potential of the industrial area became evident, and for the most part the approach of architects and developers and those who review their designs has been to build sympathetically but without historicizing pastiche. The pedestrian experience and the pedestrian scale have been important considerations in revitalizing Georgetown.

Canal Square. The first significant deviation from this pattern of mock-Georgian building in Georgetown was Canal Square. While decidedly un-Colonial, it paid sufficient attention to its context to establish a precedent for contemporary architecture in Georgetown. It connected

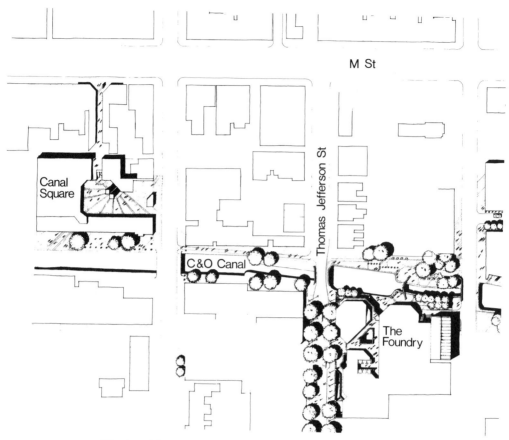

62. Canal Square in its context and some of the subsequent context it engendered. © Arthur Cotton Moore / Associates.

with an existing stone warehouse, demonstrating the value of reusing existing industrial buildings in new ways. It retained the scale of Georgetown and used materials sympathetic to Georgetown's character. Canal Square established a new precedent for the locale in site planning as well in creating a semipublic space at the interior of a block. Its program was mixed: specialty-retail and office uses.

Although Canal Square generated controversy for deviating from Georgetown traditions, its sympathetic design response to the context was recognized by local authorities, who gave the necessary approvals. It became an architectural catalyst as well as a precedent-setting economic development, demonstrating that office and retail developments were marketable in the area between M Street and the Potomac River. Equally important, it demonstrated that new development need not damage this fragile historical context. Canal Square set a standard and offered suggestions for other architects and developers who might follow, suggestions for a controlled yet still profitable response to context.

The Foundry.   Taking cues from Canal Square, the Foundry features an existing industrial building, dating from 1856, reclaimed and tied to a new office and retail structure, using similar materials but in a contemporary style. The tone of the new structure is conditioned by the existing foundry and its Georgetown context, yet it is crisp, efficient, and modern. Together the structures create a semipublic space associated with the C&O Canal. Respectful restraint is evident throughout the complex. The new structure steps up gradually from the two-storey historic foundry, ultimately reaching six storeys. The diagonal wall of the office wing helps to define the plaza and permits sunlight to reach it. Fenestration patterns are adjusted to context, with large glass openings facing the interior of the site and smaller window modules, based on historical townhouse traditions, facing neighboring streets. The glazed mansard roof (on the street side of the building, not visible in Figure 63), is a familiar local form. With this strategy the architects and the developer hoped to prove "that excellent architectural design and careful consideration of the environment are basic to a fair return." Even within a few months they were satisfied that the building, "with all that has been going on around it and in it, *looks* like it has already been in Georgetown quite a while. I would say that is a very fair return, for everyone."[6]

63. 1055 Thomas Jefferson (the Foundry), Georgetown, by Arthur Cotton Moore / Associates and ELS / Elbasani and Logan, architects, 1977. Photograph by Ronald Thomas.

Critical reaction was appreciative of the effort to defer to the setting: "The new neighbor on Thomas Jefferson Street has not only accommodated the history of Georgetown, it is making some . . . people realize that new construction, stirring new uses in among what already exists, can reveal the scale, texture, and character of a community in a telling, enjoyable manner." [7]

These two projects set off south of M Street a controlled chain reaction of commercial and residential building that was even more dramatic than in Milwaukee and Kalamazoo, a reaction that has both transformed and renewed an area that might well have been neglected or obliterated in other cities. The whole history of revitalization in Georgetown offers several lessons:

1. "Controlled reaction" does not mean that the architect is bound by narrow stylistic constraints. The Georgetown context offers at least three building traditions that architects have been able to reshape to more contemporary taste: Georgian, Victorian, and industrial vernacular. SOM's Four Seasons Hotel and Jefferson Court office building refer to different traditions (Georgian and Victorian) yet are rendered in a similarly straightforward way.

2. Although one might hope that all architects would understand a district's inherent chemistry, this is unlikely, so external controls in the form of design review are needed. In the case of Georgetown, several review bodies must approve designs. Whereas design review is often con-

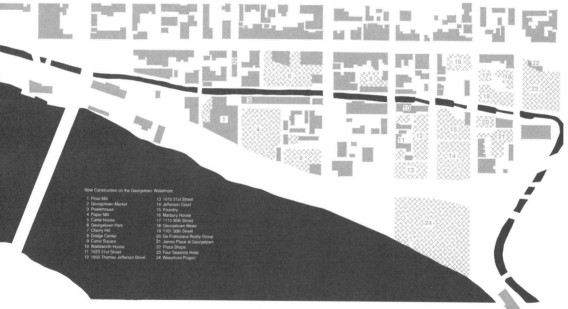

New Construction on the Georgetown Waterfront

1 Flour Mill	13 1015 31st Street
2 Georgetown Market	14 Jefferson Court
3 Powerhouse	15 Foundry
4 Paper Mill	16 Marbury House
5 Canal House	17 1115 30th Street
6 Georgetown Park	18 Georgetown Mews
7 Cherry Hill	19 1101 30th Street
8 Dodge Center	20 De Franceaux Realty Group
9 Canal Square	21 James Place at Georgetown
10 Wadsworth House	22 Plaza Shops
11 1023 31st Street	23 Four Seasons Hotel
12 1050 Thomas Jefferson Street	24 Waterfront Project

64. Georgetown, showing the addition of new structures within the grain of the town. Size, scale, and preserving the sense of a pedestrian web are key qualities in sympathetic additions to Georgetown's traditional fabric.

65. Four Seasons Hotel, Georgetown, Skidmore Owings and Merrill, architects, c. 1980.

66. Jefferson Court, Georgetown, Skidmore Owings and Merrill, architects, 1985.

servative, in Georgetown the Federal Fine Arts Commission has recognized that because waterfront buildings tend to be large, it would be a mistake to insist upon the strict historical styling associated with small structures and far better to seek designs that harmonize with, rather than imitate, the setting.

3. Contemporary needs and preferences can be accommodated even within the limits of a particular architectural or urban design setting. For example, the desire for informal semipublic spaces both indoors and outdoors has been satisfied even though the local Georgian tradition emphasized the street as a public realm. Similarly, larger windows, provision for parking, and other contemporary preferences have been included in new structures that nonetheless retain an overall sense of architectural and urban coherence.

The Georgetown case demonstrates that seminal developments like Canal Square and the Foundry can release and guide a chain reaction (rule 1), that existing buildings need not be destroyed (rule 2), and that the reaction need not be harmful to the context as a whole but can be contained while still allowing room for imagination and change (rule 3).

PORTLAND, OREGON: A POSITIVE CATALYTIC REACTION REQUIRES AN UNDERSTANDING OF THE CONTEXT

A single solution or formula will not work in all situations. There is no best form or best goal in urban design; forms and goals depend on specific situations. Milwaukee is different from Georgetown, which is different from Kalamazoo. In Phoenix, for example, the existing street grid is understood as a neutral framework that allows aggregation and subdivision (see Figure 90). But in Portland, the street grid itself is a valued element of downtown.

The importance of understanding a place is demonstrated in the efforts to revitalize the traditional retail core of Portland, centered near the

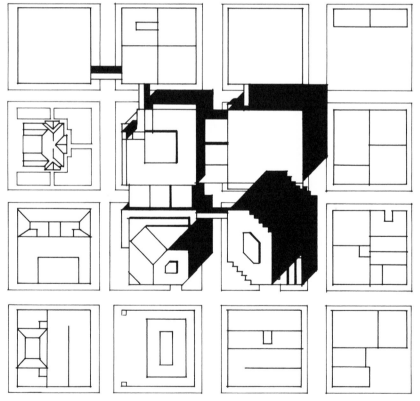

67. Cadillac-Fairview proposal by Zimmer Gunsul Frasca Partnership, 1979–1981.

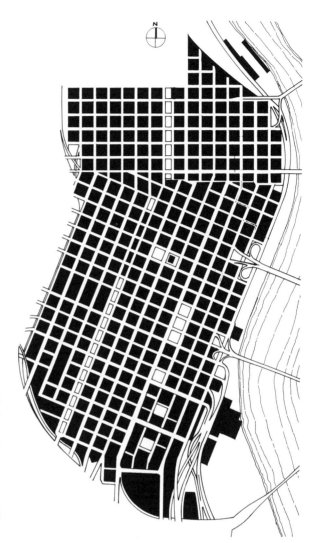

68. The fabric of Portland, with its distinctive street grid and parks, including the linear park called South Park Blocks (lower left).

Portland's role as a regional production and distribution center began in the nineteenth century, with timber as a major commodity. This role continues but has been diversified. In response to urban decay in the 1950s and 1960s, the city has engaged in a number of successful regenerative projects; for the most part, the valued heritage, the inherited urban fabric, has been respected; often it has been reinforced.

Pioneer Courthouse at Fifth and Morrison streets. Cadillac-Fairview developers proposed a multi-use scheme covering four blocks near this important intersection. The blocks would be linked by skybridges. But even though the Cadillac-Fairview scheme included up-to-date concepts and images for a multi-use urban center and would have been acceptable— even praised—in many cities, it was perceived to be undesirable for Portland. In the course of extensive public discussion, several shortcomings were identified, many of which had to do with the local context, with misunderstanding Portland:

First, the scheme seemed too much like "a suburban shopping mall turned inwards. It ignored streets, the neighborhood, the historic buildings, and the people who care about the fabric of our city life."[8] The metaphor of fabric is popular for talking about the ingredients that give an urban center a sense of cohesiveness. Portland's fabric includes a distinctive, delicate grid of streets: the blocks are unusually small (200 by 200 feet) and the streets unusually narrow (60 to 80 feet). As a consequence of this fabric, pedestrians seem to *belong* downtown; the city is scaled for people on foot. Streets are not gulfs to be negotiated. Buildings, even when tall, do not loom. Although functionalist theory would propose linking these small blocks into superblocks and eliminating some "obstructing" streets and widening others as major arterials, Portland's fabric is as it should be, with intensive development of the small blocks and enrichment of the pedestrian realm on the periphery of those blocks. Although the scale of many American street grids works against what is called street life, in Portland the grid was made for it. There, anything that reduces pedestrian use of and access to streets is suspect. The complaint that the Cadillac-Fairview scheme was turned inward, like a suburban shopping mall, was a response to this concern.

Another ingredient of Portland's fabric is its collection of highly prized open spaces. These are of two kinds: block-sized parks that provide relief from the intensive development of the grid and a linear park stretching along the west edge of downtown.

Second, the Cadillac-Fairview proposal to violate the grid pattern with skybridges (some of them wide enough to contain shops) was offensive to some people. Not only would these destroy the sense of the city's fabric, but they would also block sunlight on the streets (infrequent enough in Portland to be valued) and the views down streets (to the hills, possibly even to the city's totem, Mt. Hood). The skybridges would also mean a loss of pedestrian traffic on the sidewalks.

Third, although Portland's older buildings in themselves are not remarkable, that there are so many of them left *is*. In the last decade or two the merit of the architectural heritage has been recognized, first in the form of historic district designations on the edge of downtown, then in the renovation of individual structures throughout the city center. For some critics, the Cadillac-Fairview proposal was incompatible with many older buildings, particularly the historic Pioneer Courthouse, which would be dwarfed by the new complex. There was concern, too, about the adverse impact of such a large project on the adjacent Yamhill Historic District. Even though the design and planning controls of the district were probably strong enough to minimize adverse effects, concerns were voiced that a large project, one that violated the existing scale of the city, might also violate other valued elements of the downtown.

Fourth, the scale of the complex was also of concern. The idea of a single "imperial" (and foreign—Canadian) corporation turning four city blocks into a self-contained complex seemed more appropriate to Los Angeles (one critic called it a "Star Wars" concept) than to Portland. Portland prides itself on its up-to-date achievements, but its values are inclined to be more humanistic than systemic. A project of this scale would focus too much attention on itself, would turn its back on the smaller retailers in the area, and would threaten the charm of downtown.

Fifth, the politics and economics of the project caused some complaints. Housing for low-income residents would be lost and not replaced. Municipal funds would be used to subsidize a private enterprise.

Partly because of negative public reaction to the concept and design, partly because of the economic climate at the time, and partly because the developer and the Portland Development Commission could not agree on terms, the Cadillac-Fairview project did not proceed. As a result of the discussion, however, the value of a combined retail and mixed-use project on this site was realized, and other developers were invited to submit proposals.

Ultimately, the Rouse Company was chosen to build a project that is more responsive to downtown Portland—that is to say, one that is a better urban catalyst because it recognizes and accommodates the local ingredients. It acknowledges the elements that make downtown Portland distinctive. Instead of plunking a multi-block complex across the street from historic Pioneer Courthouse, the development, named Pioneer Place, will move the largest elements back one block and thus make the courthouse the center of an implied three-block-long downtown public place. Its edges will be defined by the facades of the surrounding office

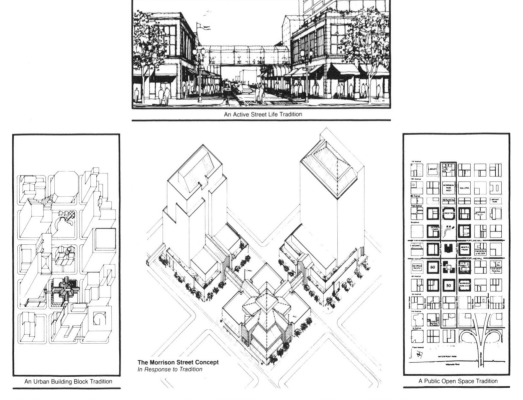

69. *Morrison Street scheme, Portland, ELS / Elbasani and Logan, architects, 1983.*

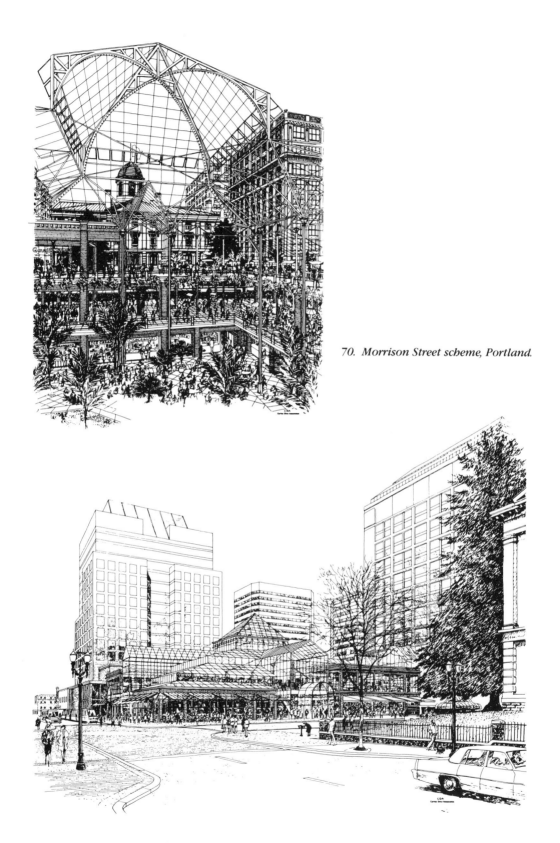

70. *Morrison Street scheme, Portland.*

buildings and department stores. The new, extended, public realm will include the Pioneer Courthouse at its center, the recently completed Pioneer Square (the city's first real piazza) at the west end, and to the east a new, highly accessible, retail pavilion that is perceived as complementing the traditional retail pattern of downtown as well as the courthouse. Thus the fabric of downtown open space will be reinforced and enlarged to include a new focal feature, the pavilion. The sense of the valued Portland grid is retained by treating each piece of the development as a separate element. Even though there are skybridges, they are as narrow as possible and do not contain shops.

OAKLAND: ALL CATALYTIC REACTIONS ARE NOT THE SAME

As these examples show, there is great diversity in urban settings, in the potential role of urban catalysts, and in the forms that catalysts take. In some situations the goal is to preserve the urban fabric while introducing new elements. In other places it is necessary to reinforce a fabric that has been eroded by poorly conceived developments and other causes. In still other, newer, cities, there may be no discernible order; there the catalytic effort introduces an ordering principle to guide subsequent development.

Many of the examples cited above are of the first type. Milwaukee's Grand Avenue, for example, required a cautious interweaving of existing buildings and the retention of the traditional character of downtown. If too much were removed or changed, the sense of the downtown could be lost. Although the strong character of existing buildings downtown was a positive feature, retail locations there were attenuated and disconnected, a liability that suburban shopping centers had overcome. Consequently, the approach was to connect existing blocks through a linking building. As a result, the feel of a downtown grid, with its traditional buildings, was retained and a readily accessible, integrated shopping complex was created.

In Georgetown, too, the existing character needed to be retained while modern development was introduced. This was accomplished through the use of familiar materials, by maintaining a respect for street edges and major pedestrian paths, and by limiting building heights.

By contrast, in Portland's Pioneer Place development it was not so much the existing architectural character that had to be preserved as the block pattern of two-hundred-foot squares. In recent years the development pattern has been to place a single major building on each small block. The Pioneer Place project follows this pattern established by the Portland Building, the Justice Building, the KOIN Center, and several other recent complexes that have a tower as the centerpiece of each block. To preserve the block system, have a single focal point on each of the three blocks, and still facilitate economical retailing, an innovative layout was needed, one that makes use of the level below grade. Thus

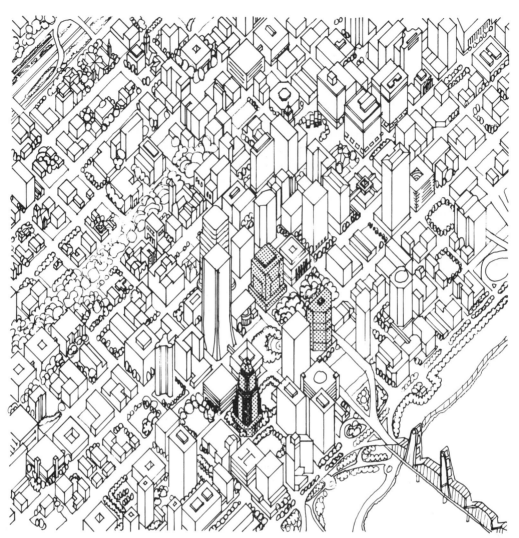

71. *Several recent buildings (shaded) fill their block-sized sites, thus reinforcing the urban pattern and the sense of the street. From top to bottom in the drawing: Portland Building, Michael Graves, architect, 1983; Justice Building, Zimmer Gunsul Frasca Partnership, 1983; KOIN Center, Zimmer Gunsul Frasca Partnership, 1983.*

the needs of both urban design and retail planning are satisfied in the development.

Another city, Oakland, California, provides an example of the need to reinforce what is left of its original urban fabric. Oakland developed as a hub at the eastern edge of San Francisco Bay, across from its more famous neighbor. Its fortunes were those of other turn-of-the-century cities responsive to westward expansion, the settlement of California, and commerce with the Far East. Its problems are those of late twentieth-century cities: competition with suburbs and a concentration of the poor and disadvantaged. Consequently, the city center is rich in the architecture of commerce but has less and less commerce to support it. Landscaped parks and cultural amenities testify to decades of civic pride and commitment, but more often downtown Oakland is known for poverty and decay. Retail activity has declined in Oakland's downtown, the dramatic diagonal intersection of Broadway, Telegraph, and San Pablo avenues. The city's turn-of-the-century character is eroding. Parking lots abound.

Once again, however, Oakland has an opportunity to blossom as the San Francisco Bay area grows. It is a crossroads of transportation and offers an alternative to San Francisco's more intensive and expensive business and residential districts. A reconstituted retail center would offer an alternative to typical suburban shopping complexes.

A city center redevelopment scheme was initially conceived as a total clearance to create a superblock that would erase not only the few remaining Victorian buildings but the unique intersection of streets as well. Fortunately, another approach has been chosen, one that seeks a resurgence of the urban character inherent in Oakland's unique plan and history. The overall plan for the City Center project has been redefined as a finer-grained office, retail, and housing complex. The earlier proposal for a suburban-style shopping center is gone, and the idea of the superblock has been partly recanted. Martin Luther King Jr. Way will be drawn into the project, becoming the primary address for many of the buildings. Re-

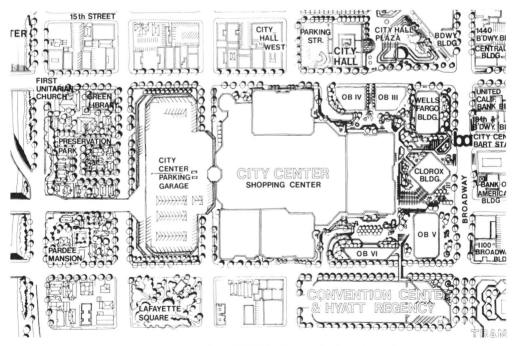

72. Original Oakland City Center design ("OB" indicates the location of an office building).

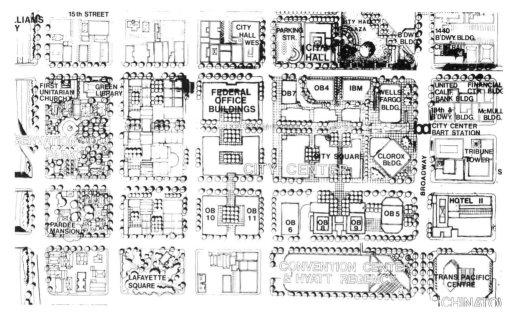

73. New scheme for Oakland City Center.

placing the proposed large department stores will be offices and a smaller specialty shopping area with an emphasis on restaurants. Thus in the new City Center plan part of the original street grid is reintroduced, the buildings are smaller and more in keeping with the scale of the surroundings, and the overall structure of the city is strengthened rather than rebuilt.

Rethinking the City Center project provided an opportunity to reinforce retail shopping patterns in an adjacent area. Because the single remaining department store in downtown Oakland (Emporium-Capwell) is located six blocks north, some critics suggested that the first plan for the new City Center misplaced the retail component, that it would make more sense to locate new department stores and shops nearer the existing one. In fact, this is what will happen. A recent plan places a new retail and mixed-use complex in the triangle bounded by San Pablo and Telegraph avenues and Twentieth Street. This scheme reinforces Oakland's urban fabric in several ways:

1. It is keyed to the existence of the Fox Theater, an important landmark. The Fox will provide a "front door" and work as part of a new plaza linking Telegraph Avenue, Broadway, and the BART (Bay Area Rapid Transit) station, thus uniting the most important loci of pedestrians downtown.

2. The scheme further re-establishes Telegraph Avenue as a major shopping and pedestrian precinct by both locating new stores there and creating a setting for additional stores there in the future.

3. Emporium-Capwell is tied in by a glazed canopy spanning Telegraph Avenue and by second-level bridges.

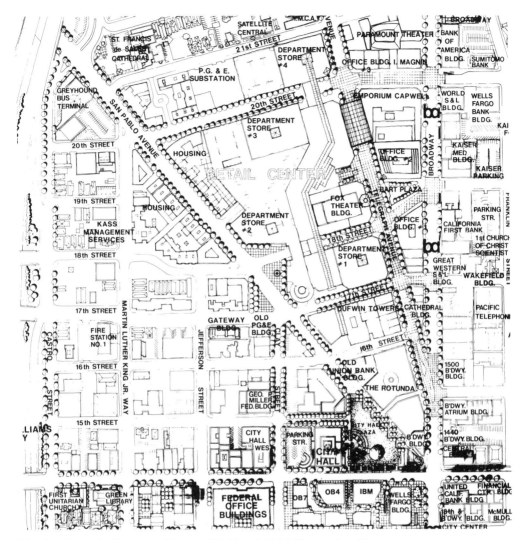

74. Plan for revitalizing retail core of Oakland, ELS / Elbasani and Logan, architects, 1985.

4. Frontage on San Pablo Avenue becomes a focus for affordable new housing, which is badly needed.

Recipes for effective urban chemistry are probably as numerous as cities themselves. Seldom will an approach appropriate to one locale work without adjustments in another. But it is possible to generalize about the approaches available in reconstructing a city. One method is to *preserve* the fabric, to work within it, as most architects have done in Portland. Another is to *reinforce* a fabric that has come undone. Milwaukee's commercial core has been tightened by the Grand Avenue. A third is to *repair* a fabric that has lost its power to order the city. This is the direction Oakland is taking. A fourth is to *create* a new format for the city,

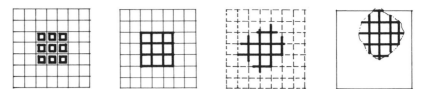

75. *Diagrammatic representation (read left to right) of preserving, reinforcing, repairing, and creating urban fabric.*

to give it a new order. Phoenix is taking this direction, as we shall see below.

PHOENIX AND GLENDALE: CATALYTIC DESIGN IS STRATEGIC

At first glance it would seem that a comprehensive plan is a prerequisite of strategic urban design. Like a chemical formula, a plan tells what needs to happen before something else can happen; it indicates what will happen when two, three, or more elements interact. In part this is true. In Portland a highly controlled plan for the city center provides "guarantees" for investors and developers, guarantees that necessary ingredients will be there so that the anticipated chemical reaction can take place. For example, sections of downtown are given land use identities. For those sections, like the retail core, that depend on other ingredients, strategic elements are offered. A transit mall was identified as crucial, so it was built first. Parking structures were also key elements, so they appear on each end of the retail core. A light rail system that crosses the transit mall was built. These are the support conditions that can precipitate and sustain a strong retail activity that will focus on the Pioneer Place development (described above). At the same time these elements were being coordinated, related concerns like middle- and upper-income housing, nighttime activities, and the waterfront as an amenity all were considered and introduced strategically.

Of course it is possible for a plan—a formula—to be wrong. Having an urban design plan does not guarantee success in achieving its goals. It also is possible that a plan constrains reactions as it attempts to guarantee future ends. One need only look at controlled shopping-mall alternatives to downtown to see the problem. Even though they mix uses, offer plenty of parking, separate pedestrians from vehicles, and give "life" in the form of skating rinks, they and similar functionalist alternatives to traditional downtowns lack richness, spontaneity, a sense of community; they are the product of one idea, one hand at the helm, one class of people. Their sound is not that of life being lived (people talking, street life), but that of omnipresent Muzak.

There is a danger that master plans for downtown can have a similar stultifying effect and that downtowns will become little more than inner city suburban malls. A key to success in revitalizing a downtown is to think strategically about the impact one element can have on another rather than to specify how each element should look and how each part should be designed. An urban design plan for catalytic reactions must be formulated with sensitivity to the ingredients at hand and should provide opportunities for infusing new ideas and the sense that we are evolving the future—not, as in many shopping centers, that the future has arrived.

In locales like Portland, Milwaukee, and Georgetown, the building history is sufficiently rich to inspire subsequent development. The character of each city is itself strong enough to guide development and to resist being consumed, sanitized, or disfigured by new events. But many cities do not have this kind of inherent character to guide and moderate development, so formulas for rationalizing change need to be introduced. Cities with little evident character, or those where growth is exploitative rather than formative, need guidance and control.

There are two ways to proceed where the urban context is weak or out of control. Where both growth and decay are occurring in a vast urban field, as in Phoenix, strategic design can *create a series of catalysts to crystallize and focus the energies of growth and to counteract decline.* Where an existing town center is redeveloping too rapidly and to the detriment of urban character and quality, as in Glendale, California, the strategy can be to *integrate the changes and to coordinate the various potent reactions that are under way.* One approach captures energy; the other guides it.

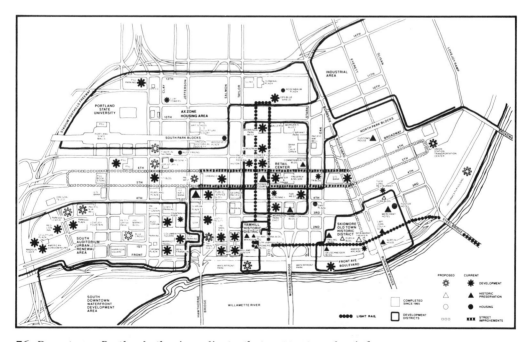

76. *Downtown Portland: the ingredients that support and reinforce one another.*

The focus of one of the fastest-growing metropolitan regions in the United States, Phoenix has suffered from the dispersal of investment from its center to suburban regions. Yet as one of the nation's ten largest cities, Phoenix has a role to play as an urban center. The development strategy for Phoenix is to attract and focus investment and other resources to shape a workable and rewarding urban center and thus counteract decline and random development.

In terms of the chemical analogy, development in Phoenix has been characterized by incidental low-grade reactions, some new construction downtown, and a great deal of typical suburban spread. As in many American cities, conventional wisdom said that profits were to be made not in the core of the city, but on its edges. The result is a vast urban field with little distinction, little character, and little "image."

Strategic development in downtown Phoenix calls for crystallizing centers that can harness unfocused growth and in turn can have catalytic side effects. Such a process has been under way in the city's downtown since 1979. It began with a strategy to achieve two goals: to create an overall framework that clarifies the grid of downtown Phoenix and to work within that framework to produce the greatest side effects. Conceptually, the strategy is a "necklace," a loosely related set of situations or opportunities. Specific development/redevelopment can take place incrementally and with catalytic impact, according to a larger set of guidelines that identify likely development districts, circulation and parking

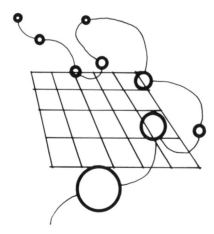

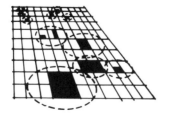

77. A "necklace" concept for development is recommended for Phoenix, a loosely related set of opportunities for development/redevelopment. Opportunities are not related chronologically, over time, but physically, reinforcing each other while seeding catalytic reactions nearby.

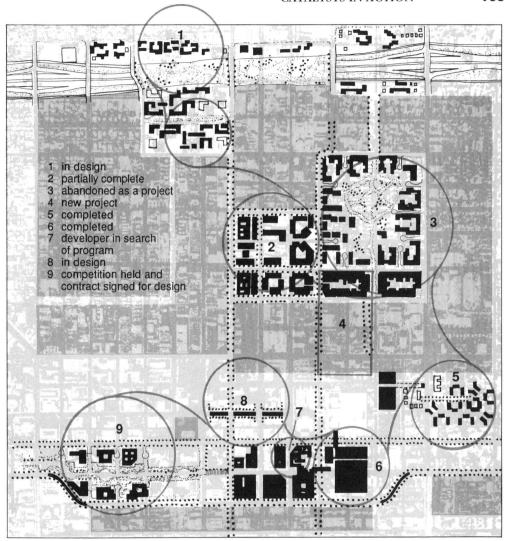

1 in design
2 partially complete
3 abandoned as a project
4 new project
5 completed
6 completed
7 developer in search
   of program
8 in design
9 competition held and
   contract signed for design

78. Elements of the development strategy for Phoenix, circa 1980, with 1987 status report.

systems, appropriate building form, and ways of giving character and appeal to streets and pedestrian routes.

The necklace concept of key projects envisions a three-phase period of development extending over approximately fifteen years. Within each five-year period a series of critically important projects would be implemented through a combination of public and private initiative. The nature and timing of each project should respond to the findings of a market evaluation. In Phoenix the projects were located in critical areas where land could be made available without causing undue hardship and where the projects could have a positive impact on surrounding land uses. Because they are identified as significant or having potential, these

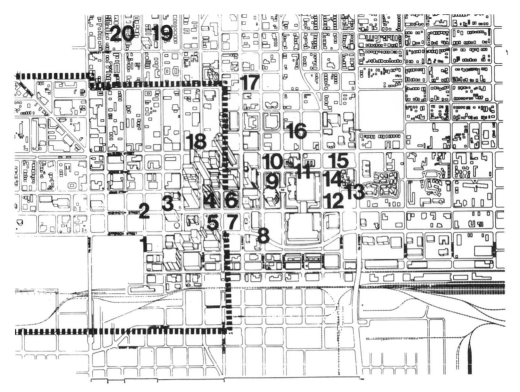

79. *Downtown Phoenix, showing projected "catalytic" projects in 1988, including a new government center, the renovation of an old theater, an urban park, a performing arts center, a streetscape program, and several private commercial projects.*

settings attract both human and financial interest and investment. Thus an anonymous urban field begins to have identifiable districts and nodes that improve comprehensibility and inspire confidence that the future is in some ways managed and consequences are in some ways predictable.

One advantage of strategic approaches to urban design is flexibility. Once the overall formula for shaping urban Phoenix is laid out, it need not be implemented in any particular sequence or period of time. (In this case, fifteen years is suggested.) The "necklace of opportunities" is just that, opportunities that can be exploited in response to need and circumstance, not according to a fixed sequence.

The necklace concept was laid out in 1980. In subsequent years many of the initial recommendations have been followed, such as the location and construction of the expanded convention center, the rerouting of Jefferson Street, the designation of a new hotel site, and the selection of a developer for a new specialty retail development to be called Square One. The Adams Street mall concept is moving toward realization. The ten-block office park project has begun. Late in 1984 the Phoenix Community Alliance, a group of local business and civic leaders, decided to inject more energy into the redevelopment of downtown to aid the city's redevelopment agency. The alliance took action by commissioning an evaluation of the downtown retail core and a study of the downtown area as a whole. Both of these efforts follow the method of the 1980 study, which recommended that developmental actions be formulated around key catalytic projects. As a result of the Phoenix Community Alliance effort, a new mixed-use project known as the superblock is under way and will play a major role in realizing the necklace.

Whereas in Phoenix development was too dispersed and needed focusing, in Glendale redevelopment was so strong that the city was in danger of losing what was already good about its main street and, more important, of being harmed, not improved, by what was happening. For Glendale the goal is to give visual coherence to new developments. It is not to design all the buildings on Brand Boulevard; it is not to set a land use plan; and it is not, as in Phoenix, just to attract development. Instead there is a development control plan that establishes certain relations, densities, and features for every parcel in the downtown but is silent about land use, except for street-front retail uses. The notion is to shape the physical character of the city while promoting mixed land uses of housing, offices, shops, hotels, and cultural facilities.

The development control plan is supported by other plans that guide public circulation and detail design and "furnishing" of streets and sidewalks. These plans work in the context of a set of urban design guidelines to make sure that new buildings, when completed, complement each other. Although some design guidelines can be straitjackets, specifying everything to the smallest detail, strategic guidelines can give direction and consistency without imposing uniformity or limiting interpretation and subtlety in individual architects' designs. The Glendale guidelines do the latter. Visual coherence is achieved in downtown Glendale by guiding the form, relation, and materials of buildings:

1. Ground floor facades should be differentiated from upper storeys in recognition that the pedestrian level differs from levels above.

2. Retail, restaurant, service, and other high-intensity pedestrian uses should be at the ground level in buildings fronting major streets, including parking structures (Figure 81f).

3. Materials used on the exteriors of buildings should lend an air of permanence and encourage civic pride.

4. Exterior colors on tall buildings should have light-to-medium values to reduce their visual bulk on the skyline. (Dark colors also increase heat gain in a climate like Glendale's.)

5. To improve overall visual coherence, new buildings should respond to the design features of earlier buildings adjacent to them. Such design features include cornice lines, colonnades, proportions, fenestration, and materials.

6. Buildings should address the street in ways that reinforce the sense of the street as a space. Lower floors of buildings should align with the street except where open areas have been specifically designated (Figure 81a).

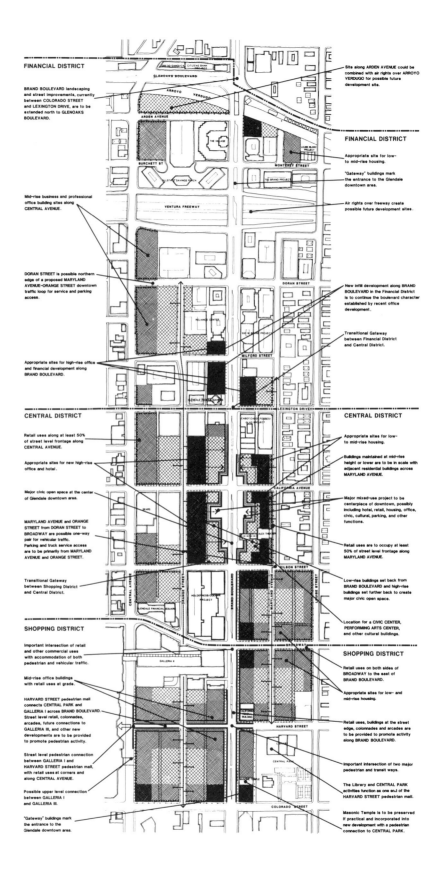

FINANCIAL DISTRICT

BRAND BOULEVARD landscaping and street improvements, currently between COLORADO STREET and LEXINGTON DRIVE, are to be extended north to GLENOAKS BOULEVARD.

Mid-rise business and professional office building sites along CENTRAL AVENUE.

DORAN STREET is possible northern edge of a proposed MARYLAND AVENUE-ORANGE STREET downtown traffic loop for service and parking access.

Appropriate sites for high-rise office and financial development along BRAND BOULEVARD.

CENTRAL DISTRICT

Retail uses along at least 50% of street level frontage along CENTRAL AVENUE.

Appropriate sites for new high-rise office and hotel.

Major civic open space at the center of Glendale downtown area.

MARYLAND AVENUE and ORANGE STREET from DORAN STREET to BROADWAY are possible one-way pair for vehicular traffic. Parking and truck service access are to be primarily from MARYLAND AVENUE and ORANGE STREET.

Transitional Gateway between Shopping District and Central District.

SHOPPING DISTRICT

Important intersection of retail and other commercial uses with accommodation of both pedestrian and vehicular traffic.

Mid-rise office buildings with retail uses at grade.

HARVARD STREET pedestrian mall connects CENTRAL PARK and GALLERIA I across BRAND BOULEVARD. Street level retail, colonnades, arcades, future connections to GALLERIA III, and other new developments are to be provided to promote pedestrian activity.

Street level pedestrian connection between GALLERIA I and HARVARD STREET pedestrian mall, with retail uses at corners and along CENTRAL AVENUE.

Possible upper level connection between GALLERIA I and GALLERIA III.

"Gateway" buildings mark the entrance to the Glendale downtown area.

Site along ARDEN AVENUE could be combined with air rights over ARROYO VERDUGO for possible future development site.

FINANCIAL DISTRICT

Appropriate site for low- to mid-rise housing.

"Gateway" buildings mark the entrance to the Glendale downtown area.

Air rights over freeway create possible future development sites.

New infill development along BRAND BOULEVARD in the Financial District is to continue the boulevard character established by recent office development.

Transitional Gateway between Financial District and Central District.

CENTRAL DISTRICT

Appropriate sites for low- to mid-rise housing.

Buildings maintained at mid-rise height or lower are to be in scale with adjacent residential buildings across MARYLAND AVENUE.

Major mixed-use project to be centerpiece of downtown, possibly including hotel, retail, housing, office, civic, cultural, parking, and other functions.

Retail uses are to occupy at least 50% of street level frontage along MARYLAND AVENUE.

Low-rise buildings set back from BRAND BOULEVARD and high-rise buildings set further back to create major civic open space.

Location for a CIVIC CENTER, PERFORMING ARTS CENTER, and other cultural buildings.

SHOPPING DISTRICT

Retail uses on both sides of BROADWAY to the east of BRAND BOULEVARD.

Appropriate sites for low- and mid-rise housing.

Retail uses, buildings at the street edge, colonnades and arcades are to be provided to promote activity along BRAND BOULEVARD.

Important intersection of two major pedestrian and transit ways.

The Library and CENTRAL PARK activities function as one end of the HARVARD STREET pedestrian mall.

Masonic Temple is to be preserved if practical and incorporated into new development with a pedestrian connection to CENTRAL PARK.

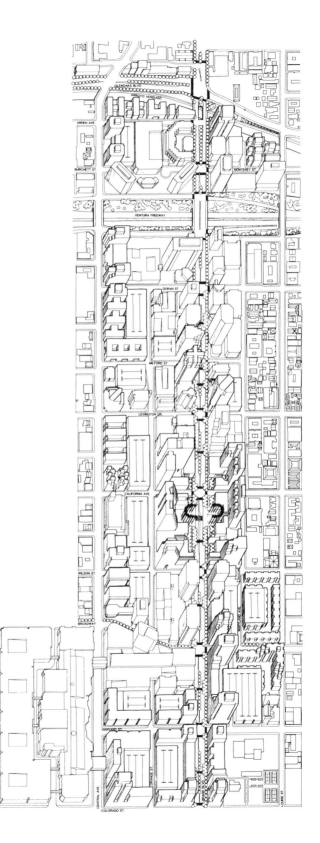

80. Development controls and anticipated results, Glendale, California. ELS / Elbasani and Logan, architects, 1985.

While many cities need a catalyst to unleash regenerative forces, Glendale needs to moderate and focus the energy that is already evident there. Glendale is next to Los Angeles but is not its suburb; it is a strong and diversified city in its own right.

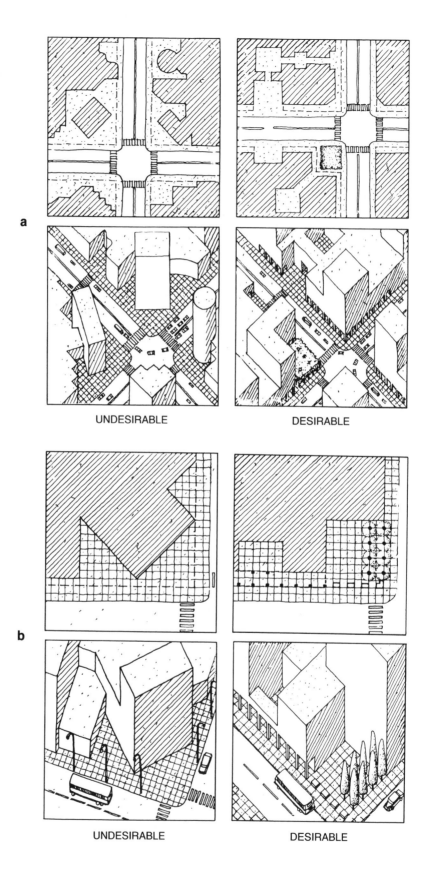

a

UNDESIRABLE   DESIRABLE

b

UNDESIRABLE   DESIRABLE

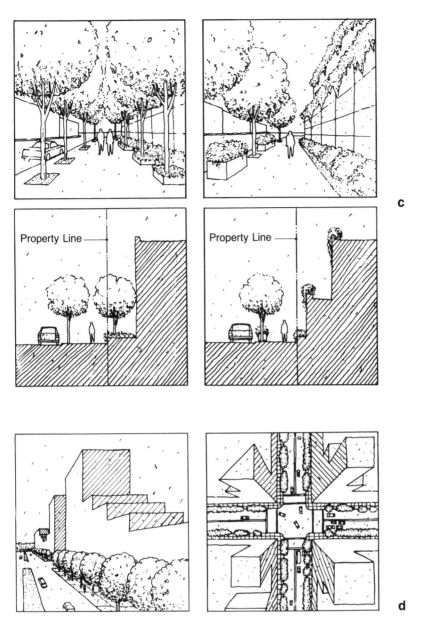

c

Property Line

Property Line

d

81. *Urban design guidelines for Glendale, California. ELS / Elbasani and Logan, architects, 1985. The guidelines are intended to shape new development so as to enhance the city center and reinforce its incipient urban character.*

e

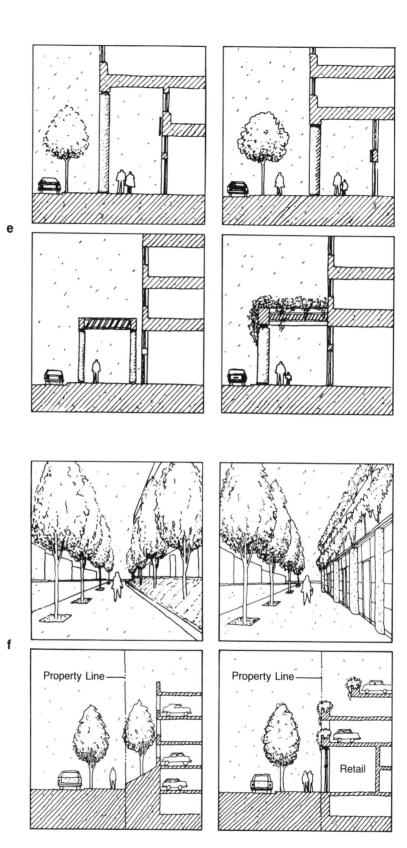

f

Property Line

Property Line

Retail

7. Open spaces, to have a strong character, should be defined on at least three sides by buildings, walls, or landscaping (Figure 81b).

8. Where retail or office uses on the ground floor are inappropriate, pedestrian ways should be enhanced with landscaped setbacks, trees, or similar elements (Figure 81c).

9. The bulk of high buildings should be minimized with offsets, changes in plane, terracing, or similar techniques.

10. The tallest buildings should be located at the corners of blocks, where their scale and prominence can be appreciated and their mass is appropriate to the scale of street intersections (Figure 81d).

11. Pedestrian areas and sidewalks should be enhanced with arcades, colonnades, and shading structures where appropriate. Alternatively, awnings or landscaping can be used to create a sense that areas are specifically for pedestrians (Figure 81e).

12. Visible sections of parking structures should harmonize with neighboring buildings through the use of similar materials and landscaping. In height, parking structures should not exceed forty-five feet unless they are enclosed by nonparking uses.

Catalytic urban design can be strategic in various ways. In some cases there will be measurable limits, as in Glendale; in other cases generic elements, like colonnades, will be specified; in still other instances the strategy will be to seed particular areas (as in Phoenix) to attract, coalesce, and channel latent development energy. The kinds and extent of the strategies must necessarily be determined according to place and need.

PORTLAND: A PRODUCT BETTER THAN THE SUM OF THE INGREDIENTS

Milwaukee's Grand Avenue is more than a shopping center; Kalamazoo Mall is more than a pedestrianized street; San Antonio's Paseo del Rio is more than a walk. To have elements of a plan work together and reinforce one another is the goal in urban design. Recognizing opportunities and shaping symbiotic relations is the challenge.

The ingredients of Portland's new Performing Arts Center would seem inconsequential, even incompatible: an old, though handsome, movie theater and an adjacent hotel; parking lots and anonymous low-rise office buildings; a striking old church and a collection of increasingly shabby movie theaters on a honky-tonk street just one block from a group of dignified edifices (art museum, historical society, Masonic Temple, club) along the linear park known as South Park Blocks.

The strategy was simple: replace the inconsequential with something of consequence; join incompatibles in an original kind of union. The union is achieved in a theater district that recognizes the popular cinematic arts associated with Portland's Broadway and the classical performing arts associated with the cultural institutions along South Park. The classic and popular arts are united by two blocks of renovation and new construction that are themselves united by a newly defined public realm, a block of Main Street marked by theatrical gateways. The activities of lobbies and foyers will spill out into this area.

Several strategies can work in transforming devalued buildings into positive urban features. One is simply to recapture intrinsic value through refurbishing and adaptation. In this way existing buildings change from disregarded to focal elements. The investment itself and the revelation of hidden value have a positive catalytic effect on adjacent areas. Countless examples can be cited, notably Ghirardelli Square, the Cannery, Boston's Quincy Market, and Seattle's Pike Place Market.

Another strategy is to incorporate existing buildings into a new urban construct. A designated-use district, for example, a performing arts district like Portland's, collects existing elements into a new form that has catalytic potential. In Sacramento deteriorating historical structures were revived as a tourist mecca that now draws people downtown. Because of its location at one end of a pedestrian mall, Old Sacramento has an impact probably greater than that of any other component of the mall. Its buildings are generic rather than exemplary, but in concert they have had a strong catalytic impact. San Antonio's Paseo del Rio is another ex-

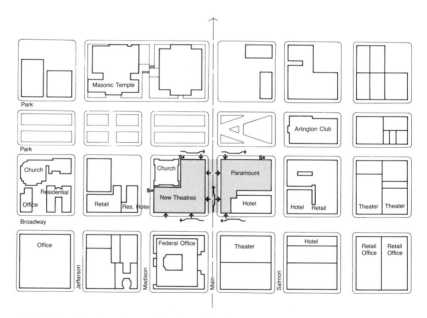

82. Performing Arts Center, Portland, by Broome, Oringdulph, O'Toole, Rudolf and Associates; ELS / Elbasani and Logan; and Barton Myers Associates, architects, 1985.
a. A movie theater reclaimed for symphony use, along with an adjacent hotel, creates a link between the Broadway entertainment district and cultural institutions along South Park. The consequence is a strong theater / leisure district composed of all three elements.

b. Park side of Performing Arts Center, Portland. Photograph © 1987 Strode Eckert Photographic.

c. Broadway side of Performing Arts Center. Photograph by Timothy Hursley.

ample of a new urban construct that redefines the town and increases the value of already-existing elements.

A third strategy is to augment and reconfigure existing elements. A web of new structures added to an existing context can create a powerful urban focus, as Milwaukee's Grand Avenue demonstrates. This reconfiguration is happening in Oakland, too, where new linkages between a collection of existing structures, most of them modest, will create a highly visible new retail core.

IN EACH CITY: THE CATALYST CAN REMAIN IDENTIFIABLE

Design guidelines, the hiring of the right person to get the job done, the careful restoration that produces a building that looks "original"—in each of these cases the catalytic element can be difficult, if not impossible, to see. But more often the architecture of urban catalysts is visible, a working element of the urban scene and a testimony to the people and visions that gave it life. It combines with elements it has engendered and takes on a permanent role. Although the concept of a "necklace" of development opportunities for central Phoenix will not be recognizable, each development will be.

In the case of Milwaukee's Grand Avenue, the steel and glass structures that link elements of the complex with the rest of downtown become a constant restrained feature of the revitalized urban center. Along with glimpses of the new, one has at all times a strong sense of earlier elements and demeanors of the city. Downtown Milwaukee testifies about rival urban grids, about changing visions for the Milwaukee River, about technological innovations in the building industry, and about the cycling process through which uses migrate yet leave valued edifices to shelter and enhance new activities. Street widths change. The role of pedestrians broadens. Cities are enriched by such evidence of change and the people who shape change.

In Georgetown, Canal Square testifies to the period of its development and the talent of its architects while at the same time it is respectful of its historic neighbors. In Portland, each element in the catalytic chain of events betrays the hand of its author as well as the influence of its context.

That the efforts of individuals who had a role in catalytic change are recognizable is important. Wanting to leave one's mark, whether as an architect, developer, owner, or sponsor, is natural, and the mix of individual initiatives and marks makes our experience of cities rich. The collage of identifiable parts is central to the urban aesthetic and the appeal of cities.

5

THE EMERGING CHARACTER
OF AMERICAN CITIES

How are American cities different from most European cities, and how do those differences affect the ingredients and formulas for urban catalysis? By examining what has been built in America, we can find hints of what to look for in undertaking the generation and regeneration of American cities.

INHERENT OPPORTUNITIES

The assertion that American cities are physically different from most European cities is implicit in the preceding chapters. But how are they different, and what do the differences mean in shaping visions for future actions?

Physical Characteristics

Most American cities are in a sense new towns and have the *orderliness of new towns.* They were laid out purposefully to house settlers coming from abroad or emigrating from east to west. Thus American cities often have a surveyor's clarity. By contrast, most European cities are organized more circumstantially in ways that reflect their origins in medieval agriculture and trade and betray subsequent necessities and events. Even those European cities that were laid out in neat grids by the Romans or as town plantations in the Middle Ages are sufficiently old to have lost the clarity of their original plans. The layering of subsequent centuries has altered and obscured earlier simplicity in European cities, so their patterns are less regular than those of newer American towns. This may account for the charming complexity Americans seem to appreciate when visiting Europe. Our towns do not have that quality yet. A comparison of Gloucester, England, and Austin, Texas, demonstrates. Both cities are based on a street grid. In the older one, however, that grid has been warped and modified by circumstances; in Austin, variation comes not through modification of the existing grid but in the way additions to it are handled.

Much of the urban design theory that values European piazzas, intimate

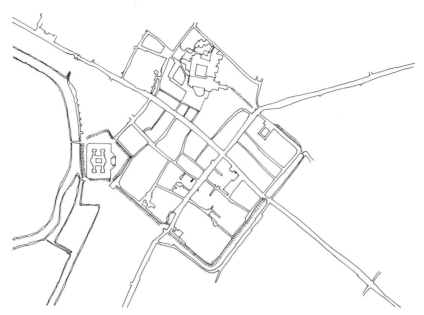

83. The grid plan of Gloucester, England, established in Roman times, has been softened by actions and events in the intervening centuries.

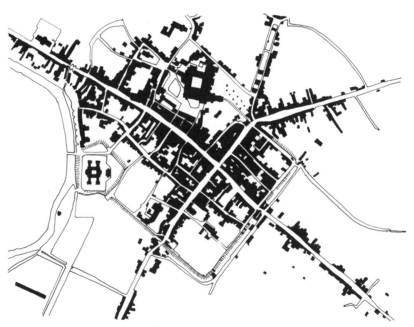

84. Gloucester, circa 1800.

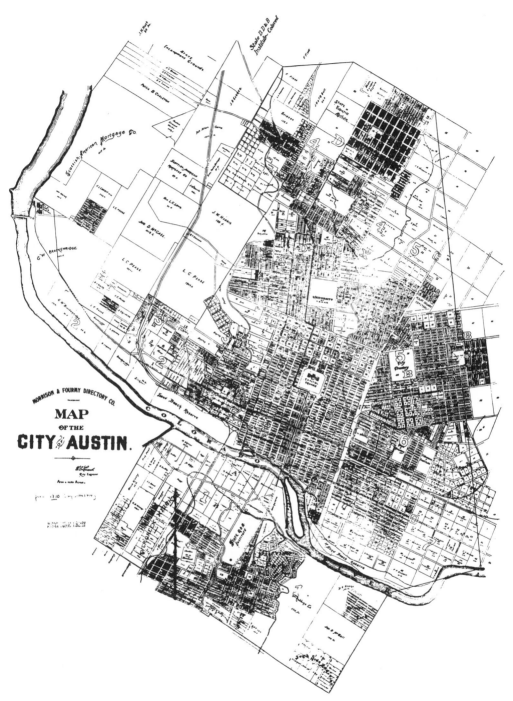

85. The grid plan of Austin, Texas (this one dated 1910), like many American grid plans, started out perfect and then became distorted. Nonetheless the grid remains legible and undeniable.

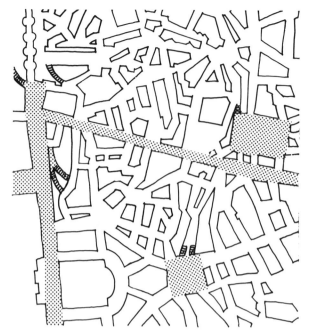

86. A European pattern of avenues, piazzas, and passages.

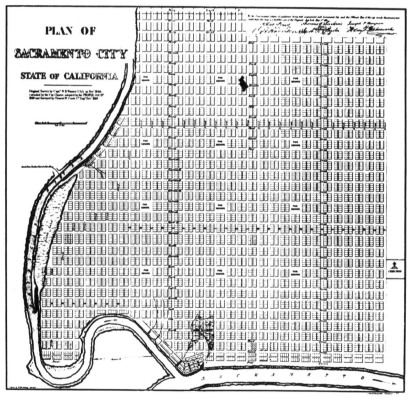

87. Pattern of avenues, squares, and alleys, Sacramento.

passages, and bold axial boulevards slicing through the irregular texture of medieval cities is of questionable relevance to American circumstances and experience. Because the American urban pattern seldom has such characteristically medieval irregularities, it has not produced such transformations. American cities do have equivalent urban forms—square, avenue, alley—but these need to be understood on their own American terms, not as poor variations on European types.

Although it is sometimes criticized for monotony, the ubiquitous American grid has the virtues of clarity and flexibility; it can make form and circulation in a city comprehensible. Cities based overall on a grid pattern, however, often come to have a variegated *patchwork pattern* as a result of land development by subdivision, with individual developments reflecting varied visions, opportunities, and convictions. Although growth-by-subdivision is also a pattern to be found in European cities, it is a pronounced and typical American phenomenon. Within center cities a variety of land uses has been laid over the original grid, creating a smaller scale patchwork of districts: warehouse, Main Street retail, light industrial, nightlife, and so forth. The patchwork of American cities provides opportunities for diversity within the regularity of the overall circulation grid. Their juxtaposition creates legible boundaries defining

88. A portion of Milwaukee shows how variegated subdivisions occur within the overall structure of a regional street grid.

neighborhoods or districts. Thus an American city can be a collection of diverse rather than uniform parts held together by the underlying physical or conceptual order of the grid.

Streets are wide and straight in American cities. With the exception of Boston, Lower Manhattan, and other cities founded in the Colonial era, American towns are characterized by straight, broad avenues. This penchant for order was perhaps a reaction to the congestion of medieval European cities, perhaps a reflection of the spaciousness of the North American frontier. Certainly, simple patterns made real estate sales easier. Later, of course, the automobile gave a compelling reason for the American city to offer a commodious and clear system for circulation.

Accommodating the automobile can be a positive rather than a reluctantly provided or unplanned feature of American urbanism. Although street closures are sometimes warranted in redevelopment, more often vehicular streets are better used to frame and focus precincts of activity. Commonwealth Avenue in Boston, Michigan Avenue in Chicago, and Wisconsin Avenue in Milwaukee typify American streets as active urban places.

A *hierarchy of highways, streets, and service alleys* is a feature of many American towns. Regional arterials are substantially different from local streets. City blocks often are subdivided by narrow lanes for deliv-

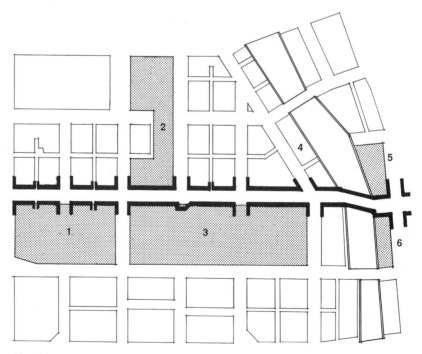

89. *Wisconsin Avenue as a frame and edge to various developments in Milwaukee: (1) the Grand Avenue extension, (2) Federal Building and Hyatt Hotel group, (3) the Grand Avenue retail development, (4) riverwalk, (5) River Place, a mixed-use development, and (6) Marine Bank (1961).*

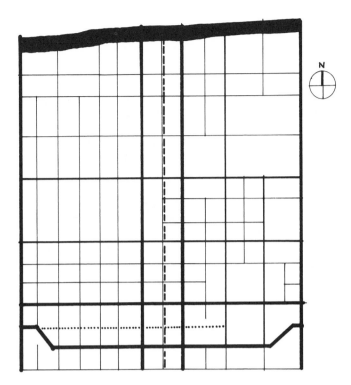

90. Hierarchical street grid in Phoenix.

ering and removing goods. Whereas in nineteenth-century Paris, Baron Haussmann created a hierarchy of streets by carving out new boulevards from the existing fabric, in many American settings the hierarchy is inherent in the plan. Phoenix, for example, evidences the range: major arterials (at one-mile intervals), secondary arterials (at one-half-mile intervals), local streets, and midblock service alleys.

Whereas European cities typically were sited for convenience or security (a flat location and/or natural barriers as defensible edges), American cities often were simply a geometry imposed upon a map of a distant locale. Defense seldom was a concern in the way it was for Europeans; the shape of American cities comes not so much from an organic relation between inhabitants and settings as from the imposition of a pattern upon the landscape, often for profit-making purposes.

A consequence of this method of town making is *striking deformations of the grid plan* when it confronts natural terrain, as at Logan, Utah, and Los Angeles. In other cases the purity of the grid is distorted by human uses, for example, a rail line or the need for a market space. One might interpret such deformations as compromises, but in fact they are opportunities for enriching the urban experience and for creating diversity in land pattern and use in the context of the ubiquitous rational urban grid. The juxtaposition of two slightly different grids along a seam created by the Milwaukee River creates unique building sites, distinctive streets, and memorable vistas.

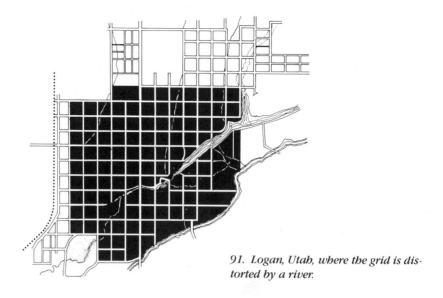

91. *Logan, Utah, where the grid is distorted by a river.*

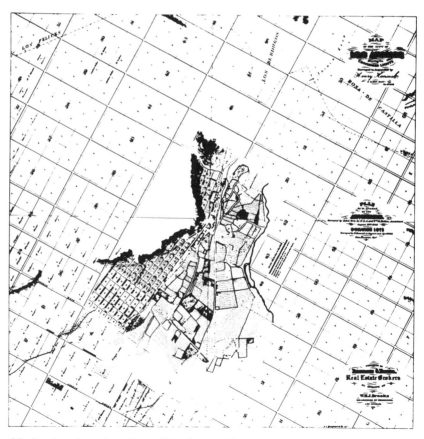

92. *Los Angeles, where the grid is distorted by topography.*

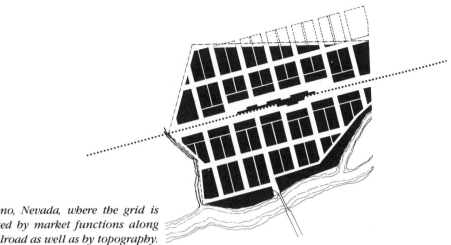

93. *Reno, Nevada, where the grid is distorted by market functions along the railroad as well as by topography.*

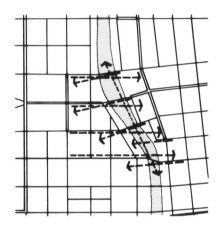

94. *Vistas and view corridors that result from the juxtaposition of grids along the Milwaukee River.*

The *architectural character* of American cities is as characteristic as the grid plan itself. A photograph of nearly any downtown or Main Street scene can readily be identified as American, for American cities *look* like American cities, not like Italian, English, or French cities. Our cities look as they do for several reasons: streets are straight and wide; antiquarian monuments are infrequent; buildings date from the nineteenth century or later; signs—literal and figurative—of commerce abound; and, most important, there is a grain and pattern to building development different from that of European cities. Denise Scott Brown caught the distinction in a study of Austin, Texas. The building patterns in Austin that she diagramed are in fact typical of many American cities.

In the United States, unlike Europe, individuated buildings usually make up the grain of towns and cities. Whereas freestanding buildings in Europe tend to be royal or religious institutions, in the United States

95. Downtown Milwaukee as a recognizably American urban scene.

most public buildings have been deemed worthy of such monumental treatment. Monuments to the market economy, too—bank, department store, office building—have asserted their own importance by standing out and standing tall. In part this is a response to the grid that carves the urban fabric into so many uniform parts. It also evidences a competitive spirit and even good-natured posturing.

This pattern gives American cities a unique look and texture. The grain is coarser than that of old-world cities, and there are often more leftover open spaces than one would like. Although the danger in this development pattern is fragmentation, there is an opportunity to fill in residual spaces with other buildings, landscape features, walls, canopies, and other smaller-scale elements.

A counterpoint to individual freestanding buildings is evident in *loft buildings* that are generalized in function and merge to form tightly knit urban districts. Particularly in the nineteenth and early twentieth centuries, industrial and commercial lofts were developed with articulated urban street facades and large, open, undifferentiated interior spaces. These are strong urban buildings by virtue of their ability to define street space, and in many cities they offer opportunities for creative retrofitting.

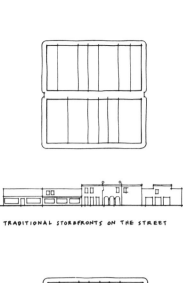

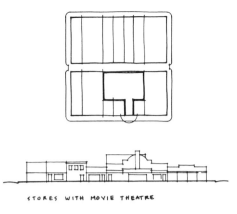

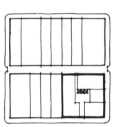

TRADITIONAL STOREFRONTS ON THE STREET

STORES WITH MOVIE THEATRE

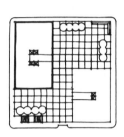

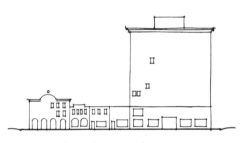

TRADITIONAL OFFICE BUILDING OR
DEPARTMENT STORE

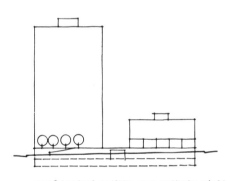

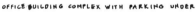

OFFICE BUILDING COMPLEX WITH PARKING UNDER

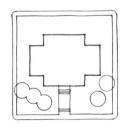

CIVIC BUILDING

96. Denise Scott Brown's analysis
of development patterns in Austin.

97. Buildings along Michigan Avenue in Chicago demonstrate the tendency to stand out, to differentiate themselves.

Earlier shopping and commercial buildings are a variant on such lofts and a recognizably American type. Stores on Main Street, U.S.A., are powerful in shaping the street but flexible, too, in accommodating activities. They can be refitted in various ways: they can be added together to make larger units; they can be reoriented to serve as modules within larger development concepts.

The *styling* of buildings, too, has taken its own course in the United States. Although classical, medieval, Renaissance, Georgian, Victorian, *moderne,* and other styles are found here, they receive uncharacteristic treatment in American hands. Hence Greek and Roman revival banks and government buildings have a recognizably American look. The neighborhoods of Georgetown would not be confused with analogous places in London. New York brownstones and San Francisco Victorians are distinctive architectural statements, whatever the sources. Main Street, U.S.A., does not look like High Street, England. The Chicago window is not found in Paris. The skyscraper has shown up only relatively recently in European cities.

Differences in the American experience give American urban design (and urban catalysis) a palette and an agenda different from those found in Europe, where an effort to create a sequence of urban squares, for instance, might be made possible by an intricate web of existing paths and neighborhood markets or similar open spaces. In North America such an effort would usually have to be created afresh and would probably fail because it would not be based on indigenous ingredients and traditions.

In most New World cities designers have another set of elements to work with. For example the undifferentiated and broad street pattern of U.S. cities offers a great opportunity to forge different kinds of streets in various parts of the city. Hierarchy can be created by changing the width and carrying capacity of streets, some emphasizing automobiles while others are zoned for increased pedestrian use. Such zoning implicitly changes the development patterns along the routes. Similarly, a "looseness" evident in the development of many American cities can be tightened by filling in and by inserting new uses in the underutilized centers of blocks, a procedure that would entail wholesale demolition in most European cities.

98. Loft buildings, Milwaukee.

Political/Economic Opportunities

Physical differences are only part of the story. American cities also differ from European cities in the politics and economics of getting things done. Like the physical fabric of cities itself, the implementation of change and regeneration here is strikingly different from that in Europe. American cities have developed much more as the products of individual and external initiative than of local planning and control. For decades American cities could only stand by and watch as developers worked where they would. Then municipalities could only stand by and watch while federal bulldozers readied land for federally mandated change.

The movement toward giving the central government a greater role in development and redevelopment over the past two hundred years grew out of a perception that only through centralization could we deal with the complexities and scale of an urbanized, industrial society. Disillusionment followed when the costs of centralized organization proved to be high taxes and perceived waste and when problems meant to be solved persisted.[1] But now the partnership of private capital monitored and moderated by public interest offers an equation that seems to have more potential for improving the quality of urban design than earlier, largely private or largely public, mechanisms. There is increasing evidence that redevelopment works when guided by this alternative balance of power.

Partnerships between public and private interests seem well suited to the catalytic notion of urban design that we advocate. Private interests are concerned with marketability, with demand. Whereas affordability will temper development efforts almost anywhere, regardless of the economic or political system, marketability is a more typically American feature in development. Is there an existing market demand? Is there a potential market? Although urban design should not be shaped only by the market economy, realism about the market is necessary if catalytic development or redevelopment is to work. Developments do not succeed on virtue alone; market demand is necessary. A strong market, such as pent-up demand for office or manufacturing space or for housing, constitutes a potential for urban catalysis.

Concern for the Broader Public Good

Also suited to the catalytic concept is public concern about quality, costs, and benefits. How will people's lives be enhanced and the efficiency of the urban system improved? Will there be more or better jobs, social services, and housing? Uncontrolled and exploitative urban revitalization rarely produces such positive urban design. The boomtown growth of downtown Austin in the early 1980s exemplifies the phenomenon of land values rising not from need but on the expectation of future need. Raw market forces prevailed in Austin. Opportunities for an improved urban center were lost because sights were set only on profits. Of course master plans and various ordinances can affect "hot" real estate markets, but in most cities these controls at best only moderate excess. They do not necessarily mold positive, publicly beneficial urban design.

Both public and private interests recognize that development does not occur in isolation. There are both direct consequences and side effects. A recent and significant development in San Francisco makes the case. The demand for housing in San Francisco is such that almost any design scheme by Santa Fe Realty for its former railroad yards near downtown (called Mission Bay) could be an economic success, including speculative development to maximize a quick return. The planning and approval climate in San Francisco is stringent, however, requiring a development plan that fits the city and has the blessings of community groups in the area. The strength of the long-term demand encourages the developer to cooperate with the city in producing a plan that has widespread support,

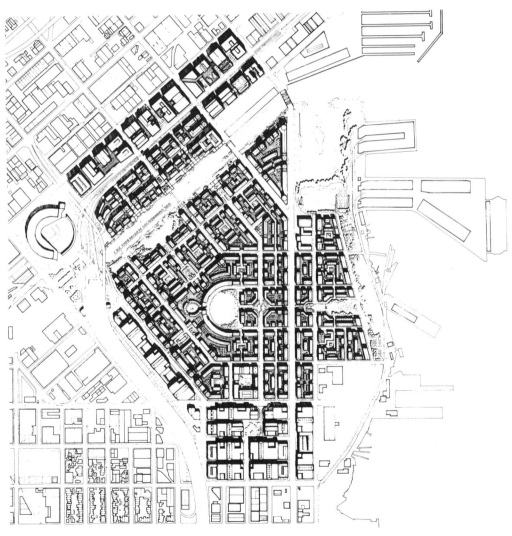

99. *Mission Bay development proposal, San Francisco.*

even though it will take longer and cost more. Both sets of interests, public and private, recognize the importance of fitting the development carefully into the physical and social fabric of the city, of moderating and guiding its catalytic impact.

Mission Bay is an opportunity presented by pent-up demand coupled with public controls. Without these controls there is a danger of unmonitored change. The emergence of partnerships between municipal government and private development capital has created opportunities for revitalization that rival historic European partnerships of municipalities and church, trade groups, or national governments. Much redevelopment in European cities could not have occurred without the financial contributions of centralized institutions, first church, crown, and guilds and then central planning authorities. Similarly the redevelopment of American cities requires the involvement of major financing bodies, not as dictators but as an economic engine guided and controlled by broader public interests.

PROVEN INGREDIENTS

American cities have produced a set of characteristic responses to opportunities for planning and development that constitute the ingredients available for revitalizing center cities. Although these ingredients are not necessarily original to America, most have been modified to suit American circumstances. In the catalog that follows, we identify obvious European roots. Our descriptions are intentionally terse because these ingre-

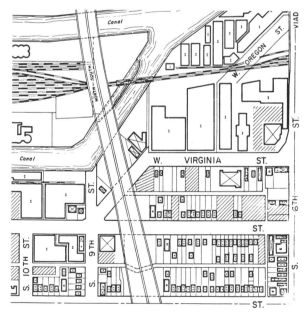

100. A swatch out of an American fabric includes high-speed regional movement, arterials, neighborhood streets and service alleys, paths, rail lines, and even a canal.

101. North Michigan Boulevard Extension, Chicago, 1920. From Chicago: The Great Central Market, *1921. According to Michael Edgerton and Kenan Heise, in* Chicago, Center for Enterprise *(Chicago: Windsor, 1982), property values increased by $12 million after this transformation of what had been more modest streets.*

dients can come to life only through their use by thoughtful designers responding to specific circumstances where catalysts, or support for catalysts, are needed.

Hierarchy of Movement. Although the principle of hierarchy of movement is established by European functionalist and systemic theory,

America's version of the idea is distinctive, perhaps because automobile use is so extensive and parking and access to parking have been a particular necessity. The hierarchy is efficient and workable. It admits the need for varied means and speeds of movement.

Boulevard.   Because they are wider and operate as arterials, boulevards carry more traffic than typical streets. They are more pleasant to experience because of their planted median strips or verges or the tone of structures fronting them. Symbolically they lend status to addresses along the way or indicate a thoroughfare of special civic significance.

Main Street.   Not surprisingly, urban elements that facilitate vehicular movement can also be places of pedestrian activity. Main Street is a major traffic artery, but it is a civic place, too. America's Main Street is a place to park a car while shopping or doing business. Teenagers cruise Main Street on Saturday night. Preservationists spruce it up to symbolize urban revitalization.

Suburban shopping centers tried to replace Main Street by offering a more palatable version that removed cars, provided shelter from the

102. Main Street, Dallas, Texas, circa 1910. In Art Work of Dallas *(The Gravure Illustration Co., 1910), part 3.*

103. Portland Transit Mall, Skidmore Owings and Merrill, architects.

weather, and expunged references to labor and to classes other than the middle class. But this was not what was needed. What went wrong with Main Street was that as cities grew, it could not provide enough parking. Moreover, existing department stores on the main street were not large enough to survive, given contemporary retailing economics.

In response, the new version of Main Street provides convenient but unobtrusive parking, consolidates sizable retail space behind a collection of familiar facades, and mixes enough vehicles with pedestrians to give a feeling of street activity without jeopardizing safety. Discordant facades are not tamed with unifying graphics programs. Instead, vital variety is encouraged.

Transit Mall. The characteristic American problem of too many automobiles even for cities designed to facilitate automobile traffic has necessitated a customized solution to make public transit integral, attractive, and convenient. Buses and streetcars must not seem to intrude but to belong; pedestrians must feel at ease with them. Nicollet Mall in Minneapolis made the first strong case for such treatments. It proved that retailing, vehicles, and pedestrians could mix profitably through good design. A more recent example, Portland's Transit Mall, is conceived as one ingredient in the catalytic chain that is rejuvenating downtown Portland.

An economic analysis was performed to evaluate the feasibility of the [Portland Transit] Mall. The analysis identified and measured the direct benefits to transit users, and transit operating cost and safety savings, issues important to economists and planners to assess project feasibility. However, local decisionmakers and citizens are not particularly concerned with the aggregation of small savings

104. Multi-use alley in San Francisco's financial district.

of time, costs, or accidents. Rather, they are concerned with using transportation investments to maintain and strengthen the downtown area. Often investing in transportation is an expensive way to provide a competitive advantage. However, the Portland Mall has met the economic expectations well and is also extremely popular with citizens and politicians.[2]

Alley.   That people and traffic can (and should) mix is a principle being explored in rethinking the role of alleys in American cities; similarly, the role of alleys solely for "service" is being rethought. Alleys add variety to the urban scene for pedestrians; they also have the potential for uses not feasible on more costly street frontage. In San Francisco's financial district, alleys are affordable sites for restaurants and office support services. (Grady Clay's book *Alleys: A Hidden Resource* describes the potential of alleys for improving the quality of American cities.)[3]

Skywalk.   Humanistic and systemic designers in Europe called for "streets in the air" to facilitate neighboring in multi-family complexes as well as pedestrian movement in intensively developed parts of cities. The American version is skywalks that ease movement and ensure comfort in office and commercial districts. Cities like Minneapolis, St. Paul, Cincinnati, and, more recently, Des Moines and Milwaukee overlay the street grid with a pedestrian network that typically makes connections at mid-block. This pattern sometimes follows service alleys.

In most cases skywalks have been added to an existing urban fabric; a result is awkward connections where new bridges attach to older buildings. When skywalks are conceived as integral to buildings rather than as additions, the visual results are usually more pleasing.

One of the consequences of skywalks can be streets without pedestrians, for when foot traffic is elevated, and when developments are oriented to the interior of buildings, streets become the province only of vehicles. If streets are to remain "friendly," skywalks must be designed and access to them located to ensure continued use of the street level.

Riverwalk. River edges, a feature of many cities, are typified by three treatments: they are the "working" backs of buildings, providing utilitarian connections between river transport and riverside industry; they

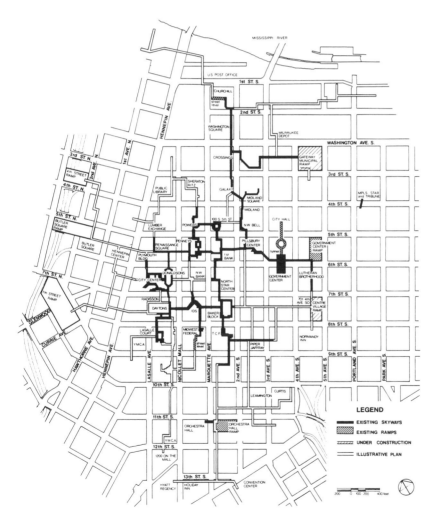

105. *Skywalk system, Minneapolis.*

106. *Paseo del Rio, San Antonio.*

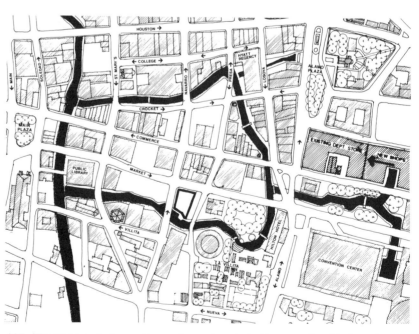

107. *The river and riverwalk create a separate pattern one level below downtown San Antonio.*

are formalized as pedestrian promenades (like the Embankment in London and the Seine embankments in Paris); they are naturalized as parks recalling an imagined idyllic character preceding urbanization (like Fairmont Park in Philadelphia).

America's preeminent riverwalk is San Antonio's Paseo del Rio. Although some of the building facades have been formalized, for the most part the back-side character of buildings was appreciated and accepted; all that needed to be done was to make the river's edge habitable and accessible. The result is a complex mix of buildings that formally address the river (like La Mansion Hotel, a former college) and less formal buildings that offer balconies and patios along the river.

In Milwaukee, developments downtown are stimulating renewed interest in pedestrian uses along the Milwaukee River. Riverwalk development, in turn, is supporting projects on abutting sites.

Promenade. In Europe pedestrian areas along grand boulevards and linear parks along streets change the act of getting from one place to another: these links between areas of activity themselves become destinations. That pedestrians mix with vehicles is not a detriment but a positive feature of such places, which "have always been like street theaters: they invite people to watch others, to stroll and browse, and to loiter." [4]

A promenade called the Rambla, modeled on Barcelona's Ramblas, is central to an urban design strategy for Austin, Texas, by Venturi, Rauch and Scott Brown: "Make Third Street both the main street and the public square of the project. We recommend the creation of an elongated, tree-lined pedestrian avenue [that] would be on the right-of-way of the soon-to-be-removed rail line along Third Street and would link Congress Avenue to Shoal Creek and thereby to the trails of Austin." [5] American designers need not look to Europe for such precedents. Brooklyn's Esplanade overlooking Manhattan "functions as a park, a viewing spot, and as a central anchoring space for the neighborhood. It feels as if Brooklyn Heights with its tight streets, were all one great building and the Esplanade were its veranda." [6]

Galleria. Although the name galleria has been appropriated for a wide variety of spaces and places, it originally referred to pedestrian streets under glass where the mix of activities associated with a commercial street is protected by a glass roof. Milan's Galleria is the model.

When the galleria appears in America,[7] it either takes over an existing street or creates an alternative place. The galleria of the Grand Avenue absorbs service alleys, and in concert with the existing interior of Plankinton Arcade, it forms an extensive, complex place. Similarly, a project called the Courtyards for Fort Wayne, Indiana, transformed a block of disparate retail units into a new complex with a glass-covered, three-storey passage along former service alleys. Kenneth Frampton pronounced the scheme an "astonishingly clever idea in relation to the disorganized, half-abandoned inner urban detritus that is being used, which has no order.

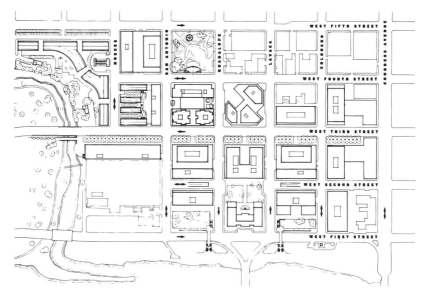

108. The Rambla, proposed for downtown Austin by Venturi, Rauch and Scott Brown, would establish a formal equivalent to a more typically American ad hoc version of the promenade: the blocks of older buildings with restaurants, bars, and boutiques along Sixth Street, not far away. The strolling, browsing, and watching characteristic of Sixth Street could carry over to this redeveloped part of downtown.

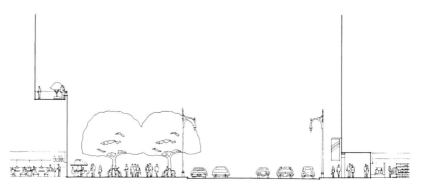

109. The proposed Rambla. Activities along the street are focused by the new promenade.

This introduction of an arcade system would revitalize the leftover bits, bond them together, and give them an internal life."[8]

Housing Precinct. The very term *precinct* suggests that a boundary or edge gives identity to a place; it also suggests a degree of security, the precinct's edge seeming defensible. Although walled compounds make poor neighbors, the desire for a sense of security must be recognized. It can be achieved by arranging housing and the passages around it to provide "eyes on the street."

The interior of a housing precinct is pedestrian oriented. Often it is raised above grade both to shelter parking and to demarcate the boundary. Shops located at grade serve a wider neighborhood as well as the housing precinct itself (see Figure 122).

Superblock.   Because the ubiquitous American grid does not lend itself to all uses, development often needs to comprise a larger mesh. Milwaukee's Grand Avenue stretches across streets to create a linear shopping center paralleling Wisconsin Avenue. In Phoenix, developments encompassing six or more contiguous blocks will create building complexes around open interior spaces. Traffic flows around or enters the complex under strict control.

The advantages of assembling elements of the grid into larger blocks are efficiency and flexibility of use. A danger is that such complexes can interrupt the free movement of pedestrians or confuse a district's traffic patterns. In the past, parking podiums underlying such developments have too often created fortresslike obstructions to pedestrian movement. Then too, larger parcels can seem to justify the development of larger buildings; the combination can make a fine-grained neighborhood seem suddenly coarse.

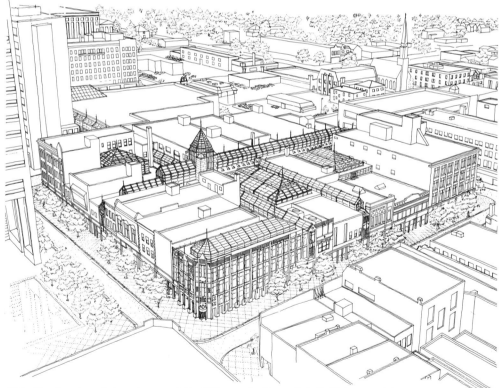

110. The Courtyards Development, Fort Wayne, Indiana. Eric R. Kuhne and Associates, 1985.

111. The Courtyards Development, Fort Wayne.

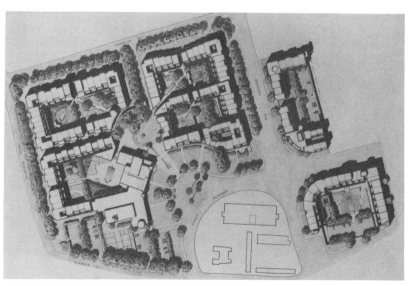

112. A housing precinct: La Entrada housing master plan, Tucson, Arizona, ELS / Elbasani and Logan, architects.

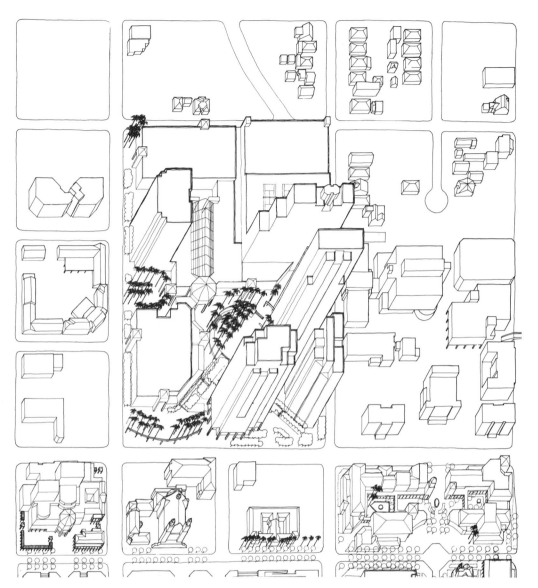

113. *Superblock proposal for downtown Phoenix, Gruen Associates, architects.*

Called superblocks, these urban elements parallel strongly Le Corbusier's notion, seen at Chandigarh in India, of pedestrian-oriented precincts within a network of roads and avenues. But in American usage they are not the underlying planning schema but are incidental, a way of drawing together or crystallizing particular areas of a city. The occasional overlaying of a larger mesh upon the grid creates welcome and often unexpected complexity within the otherwise rational and predictable urban pattern.

Pedestrian Mall.   Simultaneously a goal and a place on the way to other goals, the pedestrian mall creates a realm where people on foot feel

114. Kalamazoo Mall.

safe. Usually shops front on pedestrian malls. Associated housing is a supportive addition. Nearby parking and readily accessible public transport are crucial to keeping a mall occupied.

Regarding the success of Kalamazoo Mall over its first twenty years, a Downtown Kalamazoo Association representative concluded:

There has always been a total commitment by both the city and merchants to make the mall an attractive place to shop. There is a captive clientele of employees . . . at large businesses and institutions which ensure that a steady stream of people plies the auto-free streets. At least 75 percent of the mall stores are locally owned, a factor that guarantees a different attitude by shopkeepers and sales persons who deal with the shoppers. . . . [T]he Kalamazoo Mall was built in 1959 and as the first of its kind was early enough to attract the kind of clientele who stayed.[9]

Although for a time converting streets to malls was the most popular technique for center city redevelopment, pedestrian mall conversions do not always work. In many cases they have not brought about the anticipated retail rejuvenation—largely because they were conceived as single efforts rather than as part of a catalytic process—and the approach is less frequently used.

Positive Parking.   Once the presence of automobiles is accepted as a given in American cities, provision for their storage should be handled not grudgingly but purposefully. Parking lots and, more pointedly, parking structures need to be designed as positive ingredients of the urban fabric and experience. Although the inclination to do little more than decorate parking structures is understandable, a more useful approach is to mix parking with retail businesses, offices, housing, parks, and so forth, domesticating the beasts, making them easier, more pleasant, to keep close at hand.

City Room (Interior).   Cities can have places where people gather and activities cluster in an urban mix sheltered from troublesome weather. A city room is not a pedestrian shopping street but rather a formal place that serves as a crossroads for varied activities. The Crystal Court at the IDS Center in Minneapolis embodies the idea. For Kalamazoo a more modest version at the crossroads of downtown serves similarly as a hub for hotel, shopping, restaurant, cinema, convention center, and office uses. It was conceived as the city's "living room."

115. Morrison Park East parking structure, Portland, Oregon, tries to be a good neighbor.

116. Crystal Court, IDS Center, Minneapolis, Johnson-Burgee, architects. Photograph © 1986 Richard Payne, AIA.

City Room (Exterior). Whereas the European square or piazza often grew from earlier marketplace activities, in America urban public spaces more often have formal origins as sites for courthouses and state capitols or as arcadian settings like grazing commons and landscaped parks. Outdoor urban "rooms" where people gather for informal activities were surprisingly rare in America until recent decades. According to the authors of *A Pattern Language,* in a "Public Outdoor Room,"

what is needed is a framework which is just enough defined so that people naturally tend to stop there; and so that curiosity naturally takes people there, and

*117. Pioneer Courthouse Square, Portland, Oregon, 1984, Martin/Soderstrom/
Matteson, architects. Photograph © 1984 Strode Eckert Photographic.*

*118. Invitation to a corporate drawing room, New York City. Park Avenue
Plaza, by Skidmore Owings and Merrill, architects. Photograph by Joe Lengling.*

119. Redwood Park, San Francisco, which replaces a city street.

invites them to stay. Then, once community groups begin to gravitate toward this framework, there is a good chance that they will themselves, if they are permitted, create an environment which is appropriate to their activities.[10]

A recent example is Pioneer Courthouse Square in Portland, where formality and informality smoothly meld in a public place to which people are naturally attracted. The heart of Phoenix's Municipal Government Center will be a flexible city room.

Corporate Drawing Room (Corporate Atrium). The private equivalent of the city room is the corporate atrium, a lobbylike place through which people are introduced to a building complex, a place that also serves as a semipublic urban amenity, a gift to the city. These atria are so numerous now that they constitute a coherent way of comprehending some urban centers. Publication of a "lobby and green space locater" guide to Midtown Manhattan testifies to the new pattern in New York; it is evident elsewhere as well.[11]

The type was established in America by the Ford Foundation building in New York City. Its proliferation and its tendency to create midblock linkages has produced pedestrian webs that belie the apparent regularity of the street grid. "Many [atria] have an entrance on one street and an exit on another, establishing a secondary, episodic pathway. New York's streets and avenues may seem strictly gridded and channeled, but the lobbies, in fact, make the city quite porous."[12]

Nature in the City. The purposeful provision of natural areas in city centers has been justified on the grounds of health and aesthetics, but it can also be argued for on social and economic grounds. Park or boulevard frontage increases land value; green spaces attract people and cause

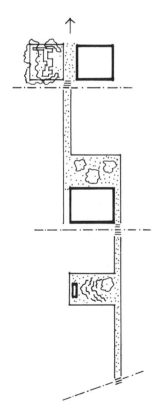

120. The Forecourt (Ira Keller) Fountain (top) and the Lovejoy Fountain (bottom), in conjunction with a small park (center), create a pedestrian link that unites sections of Portland.

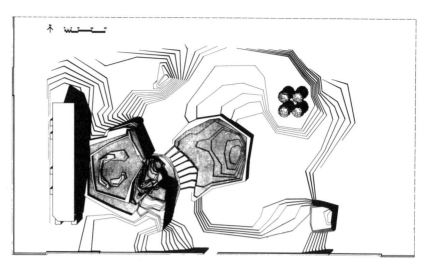

121. Site plan, Lovejoy Fountain. Lawrence Halprin, landscape architect.

them to linger. Early European examples of nature in the city were private squares associated with upper-class housing developments and public parks to provide relief from crowded living and working conditions. Corporate gardens and vest-pocket parks are recently introduced variations. The palette of design ideas for bringing nature into the city continues to broaden.

Fountain.   Although in the past fountains have celebrated their practical purpose of making water available to a populace, more often they have no celebratory role and are included halfheartedly in the cityscape. Lawrence Halprin's fountains in Portland reinvigorated the impressive tradition of water as an urban element. They are not only ornaments but parts of a larger urban design strategy:

Right from the start, the Forecourt [Fountain] plays an important part in a sequence of open spaces—a matter of great importance to Halprin. This sequence starts in the adjoining Portland Center redevelopment project, where a system of planted pedestrian malls, also by Halprin, link[s] Lovejoy Plaza to Pettigrove Park—a cluster of shady green knolls—and continues to the auditorium.[13]

Microcosm.   Conventionally called mixed-use developments, these complexes not only mix uses but blend them symbiotically. It is not enough to put housing adjacent to offices or to mix shops and convention facilities; the uses must reinforce each other. When the various ingredients of a mixed-use complex are related strategically to make them work the way a good city works, the complex becomes a microcosm of the city. Edmund Bacon argues that we should undertake such projects

because they intensify the richness of living, enhance people's range of experience and create easy access to a nearly inexhaustible variety of activities. Mixed use developments are designed at a human scale and represent a positive attempt by the development community to achieve the public objective of keeping central cities alive and making cities a viable organism.[14]

Realm in Between. Although buildings-as-objects are a natural focus of urban design, there is also a peripheral area that is too often for-

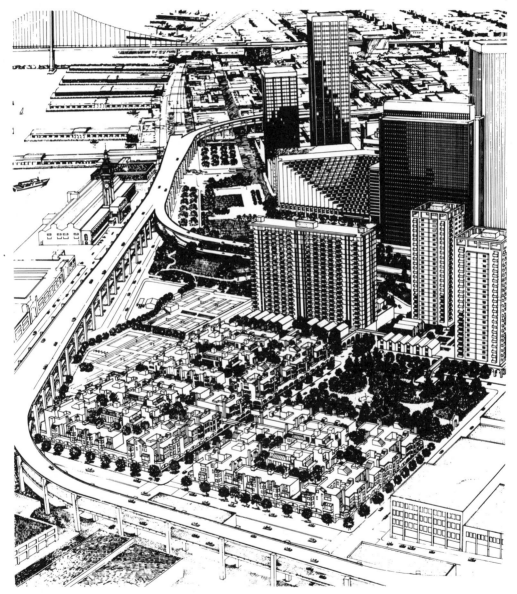

122. Embarcadero Center, Golden Gateway, and Golden Gateway Commons, San Francisco. John Portman, Wurster Bernardi and Emmons, and Fisher-Friedman, architects, designed various elements, 1962–1985.

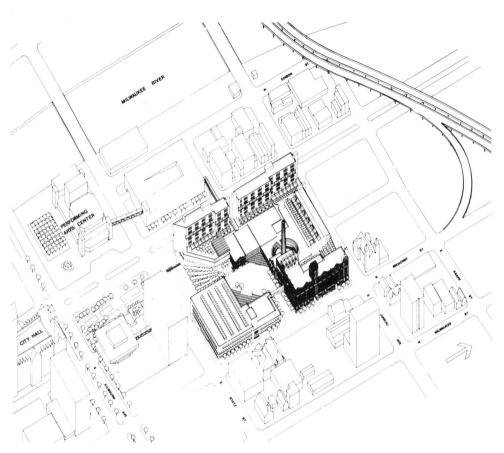

123. The Brewery, Milwaukee, a proposal for a mixed-use project incorporating the former Blatz Brewery, Pabst Bottling Plant, other brick loft buildings, and new construction that in the end would provide 470 apartments, 300 hotel rooms, and 1 million square feet of offices, shops, and parking. ELS / Elbasani and Logan, architects, 1978.

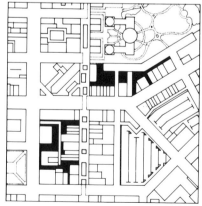

124. In Kalamazoo, the areas behind the Haymarket Historic District and the areas between Bronson Park and Kalamazoo Mall could become realms in between other places.

gotten. Between the focal elements lie realms of less precise character that nonetheless have immense potential. Between the civic center and the pedestrian mall in Kalamazoo, for example, are pedestrian passages that potentially can offer an alternative location to the commercial activities on the pedestrian mall and an informal alternative to the civic park nearby. Similarly, between the formal Haymarket historical buildings and adjacent open space is an informal realm suited to more modest commercial uses.

Pocket of the Past. Groups of older buildings with a particular character can give parts of a city individuality and character. "Historic district" is more than a bureaucratic designation; it is a promise of character and visual interest. The economic incentives for preservation created in the 1960s and 1970s slowed demolition long enough for it to be proved that pockets of the past are not an urban liability but a versatile and attractive resource. In Portland's downtown the Yamhill and Skidmore districts are crucial elements of the overall revitalization strategy, as Figure 76 indicates.

Designated-Use District. Arts districts, cultural districts, educational districts, and so forth are all areas in which particular uses benefit from proximity to one another and where the concentration of these similar uses gives an area of the city a special flavor. Unique precincts with distinctive patterns of use (Sundays, late night, early evening, and so on) provide the satisfying variety needed in a healthy city. Theater districts in Milwaukee and Portland exemplify the pattern (see Figures 33, 82).

City Stoop. A stoop lets people sit and watch the city go by. A cascade of steps (the Spanish Steps, Rome; the Opera House steps, Stockholm; the New York Public Library steps) invites large numbers of them to observe the passing scene. It is not surprising that Martin/Soderstrom/ Matteson's Portland Square design includes a substantial city stoop.

Colonnade/Arcade. Like many other elements of urban design, the colonnade, or arcade, grew out of a practical need but developed the power to mold urban character. In Southern Europe it shelters shops from the sun, and pedestrians (and casual business and socializing) from both sun and rain. Besides serving its practical purpose, it has achieved another end, giving continuity and character to urban settings. In Pasadena a colonnade was proposed to organize a collection of uses and diverse buildings, in fact to draw together several city blocks into a coherent, identifiable complex. A gesture of this magnitude seems in keeping with Pasadena's powerful city hall (glimpsed at the bottom of Figure 126).

125. *Portland's Pioneer Courthouse Square with its "stoop" in use. Martin/Soderstrom/Matteson, architects, 1984.*

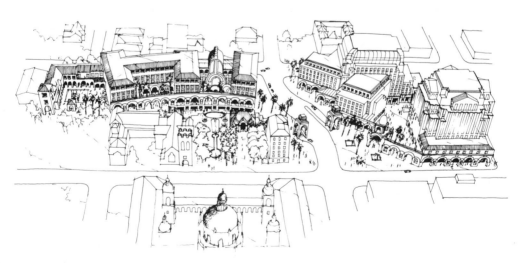

126. *A design proposal for Plaza las Fuentes, Pasadena, California, by Moore/ Ruble/Yudell, architects and planners; Lawrence Halprin, landscape architect; and Barton Myers Associates, architects, 1985.*

Furnished Street.   Whereas life on the streets of European cities grows from necessity (daily shopping, moving between public transport and work or home, meeting friends), street life in American cities is largely voluntary and much more passive. As a result, American designers work hard to make the street environment comfortable and respectable—almost like home—with places to sit, handy trash receptacles, flowers and trees, good lighting, and an overall sense of design coordination. The American view is that people at leisure will enjoy watching others who are not. Part of the success of street conversions like Nicollet Mall (Figure 127) is attributable to the quality of its furnishings.

127. Nicollet Mall, Minneapolis, Lawrence Halprin, landscape architect. Photograph by Lawrence W. Speck.

128. Chicago's Water Tower celebrates public works, identifies its district, and ornaments Michigan Avenue.

129. Typically, gateway arches have been more promotional than celebratory, but nonetheless they give scale and lend a sense of significance.

Monument. Monuments celebrate heroes, civic services, and cultural achievements. Water towers in Chicago, Milwaukee, St. Louis, and Louisville are nineteenth-century celebrations of public water supplies. A twentieth-century equivalent is a Boston water tank transformed into a canvas for art. The State Soldiers and Sailors Monument in Indianapolis is intrinsic to that city's identity. From a utilitarian standpoint, monuments are landmarks, too, identifying districts and helping us stay oriented.

At another scale, markers of the skyline, like Philadelphia's and Milwaukee's city halls, are collective symbols. And though sometimes controversial, office buildings too can become, like the Empire State Building, the Transamerica headquarters, and the Sears tower, integral parts of a city's visual image. Skytowers, with their revolving restaurants and observation decks, are the latest urban monument in America. Gateway arches of an earlier era were more promotional than celebratory, but because of their location and size, they achieved the goal of bringing monuments close to daily life (Figure 129).

DESIGN GUIDANCE

Even though American cities are ripe with opportunities and proven ingredients for revitalization abound, productive catalysis depends on another factor as well: control. On its own, the physical form of a building or urban development can influence the form of adjacent developments, but the chance of a positive catalytic impact is not sufficiently dependable to suffice as an urban design strategy. Chance is not enough. Furthermore, typical zoning and land use controls do not go far enough to guarantee architectural quality or design coherence in new developments.

There are, however, increasing numbers of sophisticated extrapolations of zoning laws beginning to enhance and support the idea of the urban catalyst. It is beyond the scope of this book to describe specific ordinances and controls that have been developed by various cities. The following taxonomy of controls is intended to identify those that can build catalytic change in architecture and urban design. To explain these varied approaches to control, we use entries to the competition for the Phoenix Municipal Government Center Master Plan and the San Francisco Downtown Plan.

The urban design challenge in Phoenix was to formulate an architectural and urban pattern that would respond to environmental conditions and local history and thus become a guide for design elsewhere in downtown Phoenix. The complex also needed to be sufficiently vivid to give Phoenix a recognizable urban symbol. In San Francisco the objectives were to make downtown livable and the skyline appropriate, "to return to the complex visual imagery of the surrounding hillsides and to the complex architectural qualities of older San Francisco buildings."[15]

Conceptual Control. Controlling urban catalysis without repressing it depends on a thoughtful choice of concepts. Is a new use district—

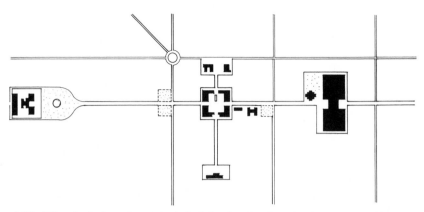

130. "Classical planning principles" in the Hartford Design Group / Tai Soo Kim proposal for Phoenix. Crossed axes link significant urban elements (State Capitol and Convention Center, railroad station and a church complex). The crossing is broadened to create the municipal center.

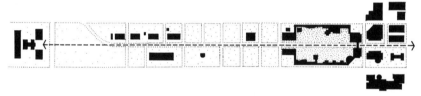

131. Arata Isozaki's Phoenix Garden and city-axis concept for Phoenix. A civic axis stretching from the Convention Center to the State Capitol bisects a walled precinct, an urban room, and a symbolic center city desert: "In contrast with the other open spaces covered with green, Phoenix Garden is a dry garden, a desert landscape . . . a perfect setting for a sculptural court."

for example, a government center—better conceived as a separate entity, as an extension of downtown, or as a link between other use districts? What physical feature is the best conceptual guide for development?

The Hartford Design Group's concept for Phoenix was based on "classical planning principles," a public space/node at the crossing of two axes that linked public and semipublic realms. Downtown would orient to two specific axes instead of to the otherwise largely undifferentiated grid. Arata Isozaki's concept was a "city garden," an enclosed desert in the heart of the city sited along a vivid arterial axis. The dramatic size—six square blocks—is evident in Figure 131. Barton Myers Associates called for a network of gardens, lanes, and courts to pattern a new downtown.

The proposal by ELS/Elbasani and Logan with Robert Frankeberger called for the municipal government center to be a "knuckle" linking and

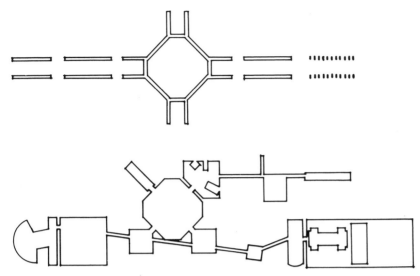

132. *The proposal of Barton Myers Associates, a network of gardens, lanes, and courts (lower figure) realized with arcades and loggias (upper figure), was intended to set a pattern for the rest of downtown. The pattern shown is from Phase 1 of the competition. Octagonal shapes in both drawings define the main piazza.*

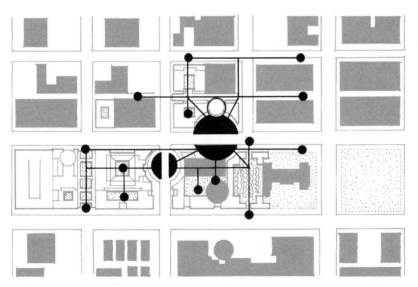

133. *The "knuckle" proposed by ELS / Elbasani and Logan and Robert Frankeberger, architects, is a concept that draws together sixteen particular planning and design features.*

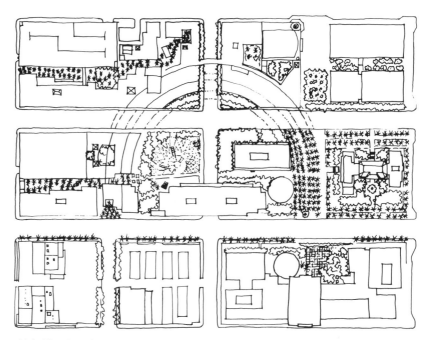

134. The Rainbow Guardian concept of Charles W. Moore and HNTB came from Arizona's Indian heritage. According to Moore, "We were happy to find that a big curved building could tie together the Old City Hall, the Palace Theater, and the Dorris Opera House; could open up vistas to the State Capitol and Union Station; and could even accommodate the big existing Municipal Building and its 'kiva' City Council Chambers. . . . All we had to do was get the colors right so that the spirits would be pleased."

providing edges for the adjacent downtown district and a projected civic area to the south. Charles W. Moore and HNTB (Howard Needles Tammen & Bergendoff) used a rainbowlike arc of new buildings to define a large public space. This figure seemed appropiate because the Rainbow Guardian, associated with the myth of creation, is sacred to Native Americans in the region. A rainbow rendered in color and texture would be used to organize the new complex and serve as its conceptual focus. In each case the concept—crossed axes, city garden, network, knuckle, and Rainbow Guardian—guides and limits subsequent design development. To work catalytically such controlling concepts must have significance beyond the realm of the initial development. For example, the crossed axes become more important than other streets in the downtown grid; a knuckle indicates two focal developments, which it then links. A network of passages could spread elsewhere downtown.

Typological Control.   Competitors in Phoenix chose two kinds of typological controls that by intention or inference could direct subsequent design. Some of the architects proposed that particular building elements were environmentally and historically appropriate and that these should become a basis for urban architecture in Phoenix. The element most frequently cited was the arcade, or colonnade, or loggia; competitors agreed that the utility of such an element in the southwestern climate, along with the historical precedents for it and its visual appeal, recommended it as a feature, even if not necessarily as an instrumental urban design concept. For the larger urban pattern, some architects proposed a web of passages connecting courtyards and patios.

Exemplars.   Exemplars are specific models, in contrast to types, which are more general. For example, two competitors at Phoenix cited Diocletian's palace and the Escorial as suitable models for a new urban pattern in Phoenix. Seldom is it appropriate, however, to model new urban buildings after specific precedents. Too many factors differ between locales or historic eras. More often exemplars and types are blended to create generic models for controlling urban patterns and building forms. These controlling models, which mix specificity and generality, often have become the basis of design guidelines (discussed below).

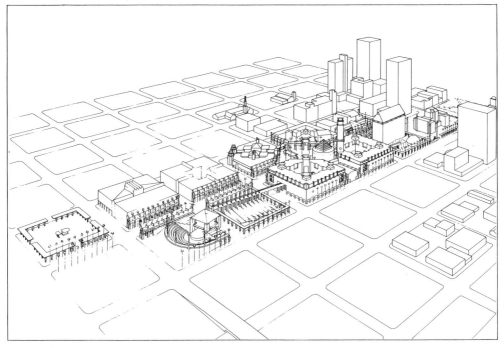

135. Barton Myers's Phase 1 scheme shows extensive use of arcades.

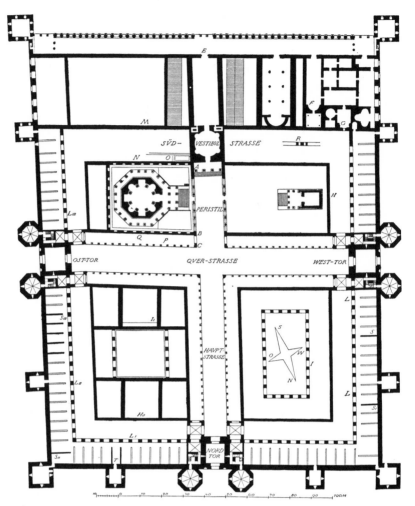

136. Diocletian's palace, with its intensive grid of arcades and patios, was one of the exemplars identified to guide development in downtown Phoenix. From George Niemann, Der Palast Diokletians in Spalato *(Vienna: Alfred Hölder, 1910).*

Norms.   Normative standards for design control typically establish the maximum height or bulk of buildings, the percentage of openings in walls, the dimensions of setbacks, floor-area ratios, and so forth. These stipulations are the traditional stuff of zoning. In recent years they have been made more specific and more subtle in response to specific urban design objectives. The Downtown Plan for San Francisco offers an example. It specifies several protections of environmental quality. It guarantees that public sidewalks will have access to sunlight and that shadows will be reduced on certain public or publicly accessible open spaces. The table describing height limits shows how such norms may be written. The San Francisco Plan also establishes trade-offs between development and the creation of open space.[16]

DESIGN GUIDELINES

Increasingly design controls are implemented through design guidelines, rules for design in a particular setting. They are not universal, and often there is a looseness about design guidelines that ensures variety and leaves room for special local character and circumstances. Design guidelines set out a body of intentions, concepts, and standards to be used in creating both buildings and open spaces. They are formulated by urban designers and planners as tools to be used by public bodies to establish goals, direct design, and help evaluate designs that are submitted for approval. They supplement the zoning maps and other quantitative standards that present the more general directions for an area plan. Guidelines are probably the most detailed design policy instruments that a community can create short of specifying designs. While they can give quantifiable standards, more often they are qualitative and require judgment in their application.

For the Phoenix Municipal Government Center, ELS/Elbasani and Logan with Robert Frankeberger proposed design guidelines as the appropriate way to direct and control development. The suggested controls took the form of limits to the height and mass of new construction and the height of cornice lines. Less specific guidelines that nonetheless exerted control called for new buildings to reflect features of adjacent or nearby buildings to assure coherence among elements of the district.

San Francisco Guidelines for Building Heights

Location		Side of Street	Maximum Wall Height at Street	Angle of Sunlight
STREET	EXTENT			
Bush	Kearny–Montgomery	South	65'	50°
Sutter	Powell–100 ft. East of Kearny	South	66'	50°
Post	Mason–200 ft. East of Kearny	South	66'	50°
Geary	Mason–Kearny	South	65'	50°
O'Farrell	Cyril Magnin–Grant	South	66'	50°
Ellis	Cyril Magnin–Stockton	South	68'	50°
Powell	Market–Sutter	East	151'	70°
Powell	Market–Sutter	West	65'	50°
Stockton	Market–Bush	East	148'	70°
Stockton	Market–Bush	West	65'	50°
Grant	Market–Bush	East	170'	70°
Grant	Market–Bush	West	74'	50°
Kearny	Market–Washington	East	170'	70°
Kearny	Market–Pine	West	74'	50°
Second	Market–300 ft. South of Folsom	West	132'	62°
New Montgomery	Market–Howard	West	132'	62°
Market	Tenth–Second	South	119'	50°
Market	South Van Ness–Twelfth	South	119'	50°

Source: 1985 San Francisco Downtown Plan, Section 146.

More than they limit, the proposed design guidelines for Phoenix *direct* future design to achieve three urban design goals: *definition of urban spaces* (the street, plazas, and courtyards); *enhancement of pedestrian experience* (arcades and colonnades, appropriate adjacent uses, landscaping, water features, and public art); and *response to climate* (shading for open spaces, windows, and pedestrian circulation; orienting buildings with regard to sun and air movement; choosing fenestration with regard to daylighting and solar gain; and the use of appropriate materials).

A set of design guidelines like these includes a range of controls. Compatibility with adjacent buildings is a controlling *concept*. Calling for building forms that have extensive perimeters and fully occupy their sites to create interior courtyards and pedestrian spaces is a *typological control*. The urban patterns of Marrakesh, Seville, Cordova, Granada, Palermo, Kashan, and Isfahan are cited as *exemplars*. Certain *standards* are established, too, like a seven-storey height limit in the district.

Design guidelines will vary with the goals they seek to implement. In Phoenix the objectives are to create a place responsive to climate that will act as a model for subsequent design in the the region. In other cases the goal might be to attract middle-class residents back to the center city or to give new identity to a downtown retail complex. Elsewhere design guidelines suggest how to reclaim parts of the city from disuse (warehouse districts, waterfronts) and put them to new uses. In all of these cases design guidelines direct and moderate the catalytic process.

Design control ("design guidance") in England during the past decade or so has had a troubled history. Apart from expected complaints that controls restrict designers' freedom and that prescribed designs interfere with normal free-market response to the preferences of consumers or users, there is the serious question whether buildings constructed according to design guidelines are good or worth the trouble. There are important differences between the guidelines for an English county, however, and those appropriate for an American city center. For one thing, British guidelines suggest a specific visual character to assure that new buildings look at home in historical contexts.

The controls suited to catalytic urban architecture in America will be much less style oriented and instead will specify generic urban forms and the volumes building mass might occupy. Then, too, they will not attempt to guide design in a whole range of cities but only in a particular one. Typological controls do not limit design freedom any more than economic constraints and site orientation do. And we are confident that designs that respond to urban types and classic elements will be fundamentally correct even if their specific embodiments vary in quality.

Controls can do more than set limits; they can lead. Incentive zoning has a mixed history in the United States. Developers took advantage of the opportunities to increase the height of buildings in return for the creation of often unusable plazas. The transfer of development rights from historically valuable structures to the sites of new construction has a better record. Tying development in one locale to the creation of hous-

 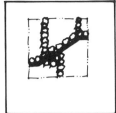 

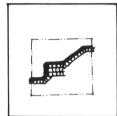 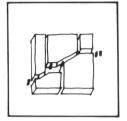

WINDOWS
Windows should be discrete openings in the exterior wall surface rather than large areas of glass subdivided by mullions. Thirty percent of all windows should be operable.

COURTYARDS
Protect courtyards from summer sun with canopies, fabric awnings, landscaping, or similar devices.

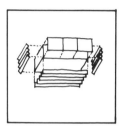

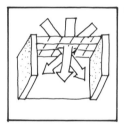 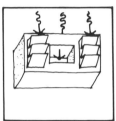

SUNSHADING
Provide shading from the sun for all windows and glass areas, through either exterior devices or deep recesses. Avoid reflective glass.

BUILDING MATERIALS
Use durable materials with high thermal mass for exterior surfaces and construction systems (for example, concrete, masonry, ceramic tile).

DAYLIGHTING
Maximize opportunities for natural daylighting of interior spaces.

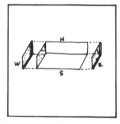

SOLAR ORIENTATION
Orient windows to north and south, rather than to east and west, whenever possible.

137. Design guidelines suggested for the Phoenix Municipal Government Center, and possibly beyond. Architects and sponsors working in the years to come deserve direction in employing features of a master plan. Design guidelines like these translate general concepts into specific standards. These are a sampler; they do not exhaust the possibilities. ELS / Elbasani and Logan architects, 1985.

ing in another and to the support of public transit is a promising technique that assures some catalytic impact.

The very writing of guidelines can have extensive consequences. Because the floor area in San Francisco's Downtown Plan is measured not at the exterior wall plane but at the average line of the window glass, deep reveals and exterior ornamentation and modulation are encouraged in designs. More typically the definition of the floor area has been determined by the building wall itself, thus encouraging the use of flat, plain building forms and surfaces, with window walls extended as far as possible.

IMPLICIT GUIDANCE

A final control, often neglected, is indirect: ideas applied in the development of one building may be applied to the development of another. For example, the attitude of the architects and developers of Ghirardelli Square toward the existing buildings suggested how other old buildings in the area might be treated. At the time there was no widespread agreement that an old factory might be both historically important and an urban amenity. But the way Ghirardelli was reclaimed set a precedent that others could follow.

In other cases a design feature rather than an attitude or point of view might suggest the treatment of subsequent developments. A strong commitment to second-level pedestrian movement in San Francisco's Golden Gateway development was mirrored in a similar system in the adjacent Embarcadero Center. The extension of Milwaukee's skywalk system across the Milwaukee River creates a foothold (a beachhead, actually) for extending it beyond the Grand Avenue. The color, detailing, orientation, massing, and so forth of one development can respond to those of an earlier complex.

We refer to these implicit design suggestions as knobs, hooks, links, and footholds. Through them developments create linkages and continuity across streets and property lines. Although there is value in an urban collage of dissimilar developments, there is also value in linkages and continuity, something that the American landowning system discourages. But as the arcades of European cities demonstrate, it is possible for connections to create continuity even where uses and ownership change. Knobs, hooks, links, and footholds are subtle ways in which architecture can be catalytic. They are suggestive rather than legislated. The architects and urban designers planning them must talk with each other about the larger urban pattern and experience. These implicit architectural influences are the most time-honored way of establishing urban cohesiveness. They are basic to the very concept of urban catalysis; their power and potential should never be underestimated.

Design controls and zoning are extensive subjects that need lengthier description and analysis. Our purpose here is simply to make the case for a sophisticated control system to direct and moderate urban catalysis. As catalysis in chemistry requires control and suggests a managed reaction, so too does urban catalysis. The unbridled marketplace can produce and has produced both good and bad—but usually accidental—catalysis in cities. We plead for controlled change in service to a collective idea of urban design quality. Design and development controls are increasingly necessary as part of the public-private partnership that seems the soundest basis for a contemporary American urbanism.

AFTERWORD

Work remains to be done to define the nature of urban catalysts so they can become the powerful city-building tools we envision. For example, a more detailed investigation of the concept of controls is needed. Someone must explain the role of human agents in unleashing and sustaining the catalytic process. The matter of visual quality—the way good design can set a standard for subsequent design—needs more attention. In the preceding chapters we have been able only to outline the processes through which one building or complex can beneficially affect others to create good urban places.

We believe that many visions for a city can be valid, and European urban design theory vividly delineates some of the possibilities. But there may be others as well, and, more important, the point is not to embody an ideology in our cities but to identify visions appropriate to particular physical, political, and socio-economic contexts. Diagrammatically, we revise the configuration of stances we offered in chapter 1 to allow all of these visions—functionalist, humanist, systemic, and formalist—to play a part, but discreetly, not by edict. For any given development, appropriate elements are taken from the range of possibilities. And then the matter of process must be faced, a notable omission in European theories. How do we implement the appropriate visions?

Through architecture that is catalytic is our answer. For us, the overriding vision of urban development is that of incremental, coordinated, controlled, and directed actions and reactions, cities in controlled evolution. Without the sense of weaving and interdependence, individual efforts too readily fail. Detroit's Renaissance Center, for example, was called a catalyst, but it was conceived more like an implant, set off from its environment by an urban moat in the form of eight lanes of traffic. The shopping complex was walled off from its context and seemed labyrinthine. "It has been an island to itself. Its design did not encourage pedestrian spillover to downtown," laments the planner Roger Hamlin.[1] It continues to falter economically, losing both money and retail tenants. Other development along the Detroit River is slowly emerging, and one day the ingredients of a revitalized Detroit center might come together. But the chemical reaction is fitful and slow. It need not have been if the formula—the ingredients, the architectural strategy, and the balance of pub-

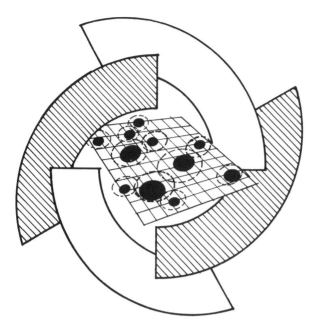

138. Revision of Figure 15. Instead of following one of the several countervailing directions of European theory, urban design in America should take an appropriate "bite" from the entire realm of overlapping, reinforcing values. The values chosen are not ends but qualifiers that condition the vital catalytic processes that are the true goal of urban design in the American context.

lic and private involvement—had been right and if the "chemists" of the Renaissance Center had understood their context.

In our view, the chemists are central to the process. Ideally each participant in the building of a city understands the workings of urban catalysts. Each architect, planner, developer, banker, and politician understands how a well-conceived, *well-designed* project can influence subsequent events to the benefit of both the parts and the whole. Beyond this understanding, other institutional tools are called for. The most potent one of recent years is the partnership between public and private interests.

Quality downtown development will succeed when citizen suggestions and concerns exert a driving force rather than remaining in a reactive position: when corporations feel a personal stake in improving their working environment rather than hoping somebody else will take care of it. And when city governments act to protect their investments downtown so as not to lose business and residents to outlying areas. These actions can take place only if the actors work together in a truly collaborative process. This is what makes private/public partnerships different from past programs. Developers, public officials, business leaders and neighborhood leaders will be *forced* to work together in order for any major project to be built. The political and financial climate in each city indicates how far the partnership must be extended—from the negotiating positions between the redevelopment agency and developer in Bunker Hill to the more elaborate public meetings in Yerba Buena Center in San Francisco and the Whittier neighborhood in Minneapolis.[2]

Some critics argue that the partnership of public power and private investment should be avoided, that it is wrong for private investors to profit from the substantial public subsidies that typically are needed to achieve urban revitalization. But apart from the counter-argument that the checks and balances of public and private investment are beneficial, there is another compelling argument against the critics' position: center city redevelopment cannot happen in any other way in America now. Private initiative and investment are needed to create settings for office work, shopping, industrial production, servicing, entertainment, and habitation. Investors have, essentially, two options: to build in the center city by redeveloping it or to build on vacant suburban land. From a financial standpoint, the suburban setting is the rational choice unless public subsidies are offered for the redevelopment of center city sites because (1) assembling land in the city typically means negotiating with multiple land owners, whereas developers of suburban sites can typically negotiate with a single owner; (2) the historic preservation lobby is active and powerful in most cities, whereas there is little to save and less political organization in suburban areas; and (3) the politics of the center city are more complicated, and development there is more costly. Ethnic, class, and business interest groups compete for residual development benefits. Redevelopment in the center city often requires assurances of jobs for and equity participation by minorities. And land costs and taxes are higher.

Thus redevelopment can be economically and politically feasible in the center city only if public power works in concert with private development. In the case of San Diego, for example, private investment would not have occurred without public investment and commitments to smooth the way for redevelopment. Furthermore, the city's power to redevelop was severely limited; it needed private initiatives. As a result, several actors now work together: "Though the city, so far, has been a catalyst and contributor, real momentum toward rehabilitation is developing in the private sector."[3]

The foregoing explanation for the difficulty of urban redevelopment is similar to the classic argument for government intervention in cities, the justification for the federal bulldozer. But now the problem is approached with more finesse and skill. The difference is like that between the crude amputative surgery of the nineteenth century and today's laser-assisted surgery. The new private redevelopment corporations, which are needed to mediate between public and private actions, are one reason for the change. In Milwaukee, the mediator was the Milwaukee Redevelopment Corporation; in Phoenix, the Phoenix Community Alliance; in San Diego, the Centre City Development Corporation (CCDC). Gerald M. Trimble, as executive director of the CCDC, called the organization a "broker." It finds areas of mutual interest between public and private sectors and provides impetus to move ahead and forge alliances. It sets up a positive climate in which the desired reactions take place. In addition to bringing actors together and initiating action, it can also have a moderating effect. In San Diego, for example, the CCDC engages in design review.[4]

Although the development corporation is easily seen as a catalyst in various cities, it is just as easily seen as the chemist who orchestrates the catalysis, arranging for the appropriate catalytic agent—the key architectural element—to be set in motion. Still, however useful a development corporation may be in the process, it is not necessarily the only chemist possible. We can imagine equally effective initiative and guidance from a consortium of owners, or a trust, or other groups, any of which could bring together actors, elements, and controls that will capitalize on the opportunities in a district or a downtown and, through architectural design, set in motion an appropriate catalytic reaction.

American cities are different from cities elsewhere in the world, and our theory of urban design must reflect the differences. Every designer of buildings or open spaces must become a student of the American city and the ingredients that make it unique. It may not be necessary to learn to love Las Vegas, but it is important to understand its similarities to, say, Cincinnati. A knowledge of our own urban heritage, a dash of healthy pragmatism, a sense of our European roots and the values embodied in European theory, and a desire to play the chemist can produce a truly catalytic architecture for a truly American urbanism.

NOTES

PREFACE

1. Jane Jacobs, *The Death and Life of Great American Cities* (New York: Random House, 1961).
2. Jonathan Barnett, *An Introduction to Urban Design* (New York: Harper & Row, 1982).
3. For example, Edmund N. Bacon, *The Design of Cities,* rev. ed. (New York: Penguin, 1974).
4. Jonathan Barnett, *The Elusive City* (New York: Harper & Row, 1982), 193.

CHAPTER 1

1. José Luis Sert, "Centres of Community Life," in Jaqueline Tyrwhitt, José Luis Sert, and Ernesto N. Rogers, eds., *CIAM 8: The Heart of the City* (London: Lund Humphries, 1952), 11.
2. "A Short Outline of the Core, Extracts from Statements Prepared during the Eighth Congress of CIAM," in Jaqueline Tyrwhitt et al., *CIAM 8,* p. 165.
3. Ibid.
4. Ibid., 164.
5. Charles Edouard Jeanneret-Gris, *The Athens Charter* (New York: Grossman, 1973), part 84.
6. Constantine A. Doxiadis, *Urban Renewal and the Future of the American City* (Chicago: Public Administration Service, 1966), 157–59.
7. Jane Jacobs, *The Death and Life of Great American Cities* (New York: Random House, 1961), 25.
8. Oscar Hansen, quoted in Alison Smithson, ed., *Team 10 Primer* (Cambridge: MIT Press, 1968), 45.
9. Aldo Rossi, *The Architecture of the City* (Cambridge: MIT Press, 1982), 118.
10. CIAM 9, Aix-en-Provence, 24 July 1953, quoted in Smithson, *Team 10 Primer,* 78.
11. Leon Krier, "The Reconstruction of the City," in *Rational Architecture* (Brussels: Editions des Archives d'Architecture Moderne, 1978), 41.
12. Rossi, *The Architecture of the City,* 55.
13. Ibid., 48.
14. Aldo van Eyck, "Place and Occasion," *Progressive Architecture* 43 (September 1962):155.

15. Herman Hertzberger, "Structuralism—a New Trend in Architecture," *Bauen + Wohnen* 30 (January 1976):23.

16. Jane Jacobs, in *The Exploding Metropolis* (Garden City, N.Y.: Doubleday, 1958), 160.

17. Jacobs, *Death and Life,* 14.

18. Aldo van Eyck, quoted in Oscar Newman, *CIAM '59 in Otterloo* (Stuttgart: Karl Krämer, 1961), 27.

19. Aldo van Eyck, quoted in Smithson, *Team 10 Primer,* 43.

20. Gordon Cullen, *The Concise Townscape* (London: Architectural Press, 1971), 8.

21. Donald Appleyard with M. Sue Gerson and Mark Lintell, *Livable Streets* (Berkeley: University of California Press, 1981); Bernard Rudofsky, *Streets for People* (Garden City, N.Y.: Doubleday, 1969).

22. Alison Smithson and Peter Smithson, *Team 10 Primer,* 78, 82.

23. Donald Appleyard and Mark Lintell, "Environmental Quality of City Streets," Working Paper no. 142, Institute of Urban and Regional Development, University of California, Berkeley, December 1970.

24. In Alison Smithson, *Team 10 Primer,* 22.

25. Jane Jacobs, in *The Exploding Metropolis,* 158.

26. Colin Rowe and Fred Koetter, *Collage City* (Cambridge: MIT Press, 1978).

27. Smithson, *Team 10 Primer,* 48.

28. Alison Smithson and Peter Smithson, "Uppercase," in *Team 10 Primer,* 48.

29. N. J. Habraken, J. Th. Boekholt, P.J.M. Dinjens, and A. P. Thijssen, *Variations: The Systematic Design of Supports* (Cambridge: Laboratory of Architecture and Planning at MIT, 1976), 21.

30. *Forum* (Holland) 7 (1959), quoted in Smithson, *Team 10 Primer,* 52.

31. Udo Kultermann, ed., *Kenzo Tange, 1946–1969* (London: Pall Mall, 1970), 241.

32. Arnulf Lüchinger, *Structuralism in Architecture and Urban Planning* (Stuttgart: Karl Krämer, 1981), 15.

33. Ibid., 31.

34. Smithson, *Team 10 Primer,* 62.

35. *Forum* (Holland) 7 (1959), quoted in Smithson, *Team 10 Primer,* 52.

36. Leon Krier, in *Rational Architecture,* 41.

37. Anthony Vidler, "The Third Typology," in *Rational Architecture,* 29.

38. Rossi, *The Architecture of the City,* 64.

39. Deborah Berke, in *Rob Krier: Urban Projects, 1968–82, Catalogue 5* (New York: Rizzoli and Institute for Architecture and Urban Studies, 1982) 11.

40. CIAM 1928 meeting at La Sarraz.

41. Jacobs, *Death and Life,* 15, 14.

42. See the discussion of formalist design in Berke, *Rob Krier: Urban Projects,* 13.

43. See the account of Friedrich Achleitner's ideas in *Rob Krier on Architecture* (London: Academy, 1982), 7.

44. Ibid.

45. Berke, in *Rob Krier: Urban Projects,* 12.

CHAPTER 2

1. Clarence S. Stein, *Toward New Towns for America* (Liverpool: University Press, 1951), 194–95.

2. Hamid Shirvani, *The Urban Design Process* (New York: Van Nostrand Reinhold, 1985).

3. Kevin Lynch, *A Theory of Good City Form* (Cambridge: MIT Press, 1981).

4. Christopher Alexander, Hajo Neis, Aremis Anninou, and Ingrid King, *A New Theory of Urban Design* (New York: Oxford University Press, 1987).

5. Frank Lloyd Wright, *The Living City* (New York: Bramhall House, 1958), 83.

6. Wayne Attoe and Mark Latus, "The First Public Housing," *Journal of Popular Culture* (Summer 1976): 142–49.

7. Edmund N. Bacon, *The Design of Cities,* rev. ed. (New York: Penguin, 1974), 33–35.

8. Ibid.

9. Jonathan Barnett, *An Introduction to Urban Design* (New York: Harper & Row, 1982), 6.

10. Ibid., 12.

11. Aldo Rossi, *The Architecture of the City* (Cambridge: MIT Press, 1982), 69.

12. Rodrigo Perez de Arce, *Urban Transformations* (London: Architectural Association Exhibition Catalog, April–May 1980).

CHAPTER 3

1. Stephen F. Dragos, "Privately Funded Mechanisms for Milwaukee Redevelopment," *Urban Land* 36, no. 1 (January 1977): 21.

2. Gay Williams, New York Times News Service, published in *Gainesville Sun,* 3 October 1982.

3. Ann Lamboley, "Fairest of the Malls," *Isthmus of Madison* 8, no. 27 (8–14 July 1983): 1.

4. Stephen F. Dragos, quoted in *Business Journal,* 26 March 1984.

5. Stephen F. Dragos, *Baltimore Sun,* 5 July 1983.

6. *Milwaukee Sentinel,* 27 April 1983.

7. Helen Pauley, "Renaissance Man," *Milwaukee Magazine* (August 1985): 46.

8. Dragos, quoted in Lamboley, "Fairest of the Malls," 10.

9. Pauley, "Renaissance Man," 46.

10. *Milwaukee Journal,* 23 October 1983.

11. Stephen F. Dragos, *Business Journal,* 26 March 1984, 21.

12. Dragos, quoted in Lamboley, "Fairest of the Malls," 9.

13. *Milwaukee Journal,* 18 March 1984.

14. *Urban Land Institute,* Reference File 13, no. 3.

15. Paula Boyd, quoted in Lamboley, "Fairest of the Malls," 1.

16. Dragos, *Business Journal.*

17. *Milwaukee Journal,* 29 April 1984.

18. George Mitchell, quoted in *Milwaukee Journal,* 4 March 1984. Mitchell represented the Carley Capital Group, the developer that built the Federal Building in Milwaukee. One reason they agreed to be involved was the availability of tax increment financing.

19. Stephen F. Dragos, *Milwaukee Journal,* 7 September 1982.

20. Editorial, WTMJ Television, 26 August 1982.

21. Stephen F. Dragos, *Milwaukee Journal,* 7 September 1982.

22. Discussions of what might be called the behavioral/political element in urban revitalization may be found in R. Scott Fosler and Renee A. Berger, *Public-Private Partnerships in American Cities: Seven Case Studies* (Lexington, Mass.: Lexington Books, 1982).

CHAPTER 4

1. For a description of the first two decades of downtown revitalization in Kalamazoo, see Louis B. Schlivek, "Kalamazoo," *American Institute of Architects Journal* (August 1975): 17–25.

2. Victor Gruen, address to the National Municipal League's National Conference on Government, November 1959.

3. *Kalamazoo Gazette,* Supplement, 1 January 1980.

4. Suzanne Stephens, *Progressive Architecture* 57 (May 1976): 69.

5. Kalamazoo Downtown Development Authority, *Work Program: 1982–83,* October 1982, 2.

6. Paul Upchurch, general manager for Inland Steel Development Corporation, quoted in *Architectural Record* 161 (February 1977): 102.

7. William Marlin, *Architectural Record* 161 (February 1977): 96, 102.

8. Richard W. Norman, *Oregon Journal,* 15 April 1982.

CHAPTER 5

1. R. Scott Fosler and Renee A. Berger, eds., *Public-Private Partnerships in American Cities: Seven Case Studies* (Lexington, Mass.: Lexington Books, 1982), 4–5.

2. Kenneth J. Dueker and Pete Pendleton, "Evaluation of the Portland Transit Mall" (Portland, Oreg.: Center for Urban Studies, Portland State University, January 1983), 26–27.

3. Grady Clay, *Alleys: A Hidden Resource* (Louisville, Ky.: Grady Clay & Co., 1978).

4. Christopher Alexander, Sara Ishikawa, and Murray Silverstein, with Max Jacobson, Ingrid Fiksdahl-King, and Shlomo Angel, *A Pattern Language* (New York: Oxford University Press, 1977), 169.

5. Denise Scott Brown, "Visions of the Future Based on Lessons from the Past," *Center* 1 (1985):60.

6. Paul Goldberger, *New York Times,* 14 November 1986, 23.

7. This description is drawn from American usage. For a cross-cultural perspective that links gallerias to arcades and much more, see Johann Friedrich Geist, *Arcades: The History of a Building Type* (Cambridge: MIT Press, 1983); see also Richard Saxon, *Atrium Buildings* (London: Architectural Press, 1983).

8. Kenneth Frampton, "The Courtyards," *Progressive Architecture* 66 (January 1985): 110.

9. Carol Roberts, quoted in *Kalamazoo Gazette,* 1 January 1980, 29.

10. Alexander et al., *A Pattern Language,* 350.

11. Joseph Giovannini, *New York Times,* 9 March 1984, 18, 17.

12. Ibid.

13. "Portland's Walk-In Waterfall," *Architectural Forum* 133 (October 1970): 56.

14. Edmund Bacon, quoted in Robert E. Witherspoon, Jon P. Abbett, and Robert M. Gladstone, *Mixed-Use Developments: New Ways of Land Use* (Washington, D.C.: Urban Land Institute, 1976), 3.

15. City and County of San Francisco, "Downtown Plan," 17 October 1985.

16. Ibid.

AFTERWORD

1. Quoted in Isabel Wilkerson, "Detroit's Symbol of Revival Now Epitomizes Its Problems," *New York Times,* 1 September 1986, 6.

2. Will Fleissig, "How Partnerships Encourage Revitalization," *Urban Design International* 4, no. 1 (Fall 1982): 12.

3. *San Diego Transcript,* 27 December 1977.

4. Interview with Gerald M. Trimble, October 1986.

INDEX

Accretion, Milwaukee, 71
Activities. *See* Uses
Adams Street mall, Phoenix, 110
Adaptive reuse, xiii, 85–86, 92, 118
Aesthetics: American practice and, 19;
  formalist stance and, 16; industrial, 10,
  13, 70, 94. *See also* City vision; Styling;
  Theory, urban design
Alexander, Christopher, 19, 20
Alleys: in American cities, 140; in street
  hierarchy, 126–27
Alleys (Clay), 140
American cities: American distinctiveness
  and, ix–xi, 44, 121–70, 174; American
  theory of design for, ix–xi, xii–xiv, 19,
  42–43, 44, 174; decline of center in,
  21; European influence on design practice in, 18, 19–40, 44, 140, 143, 154,
  157, 174; ingredients for revitalization
  of, 136–61; motivations for improvement of center of, 21; physical characteristics of, 121–33; pragmatism in
  design of, xiv, 40–43
Anthropological structuralism, 12
Arcades, 39–40, 143–44, 157, 164, 165,
  170. *See also* Plankinton Arcade,
  Milwaukee
Arcadia Creek, Kalamazoo, 81–84
Arches, gateway, 160, 161
Architecture: of American cities, 129–33;
  catalytic, xi, xiii–xiv, 46, 91–92, 120,
  168–70, 171, 174; in Milwaukee,
  63–66, 69; pragmatism and, 43; styles
  of, 94–95, 132–33. *See also* Historically significant buildings/
  neighborhoods
Athens Charter, CIAM, 1–2, 5, 17
Austin, Texas: American character of,
  ix–x, 129; development patterns in,
  131; grid of, 121, 123; market forces
  in, 134; Rambla, 143, 144; Sixth Street,
  144
Automobile traffic. *See* Vehicular traffic

Bacon, Edmund, 19, 33–34, 37, 40, 58,
  154–55
Bakema, Jacob, 5n
Baltimore, renaissance in, 40
Barcelona, Ramblas, 143
Barnett, Jonathan, xi, xv, 19, 20, 40–41
Barton-Aschman Associates, 77
Bauhaus, 1, 21
Beaux-Arts design, 13–15, 16, 35, 36–
  37. *See also* Formalist stance
Beckley, Robert M., 73
Berne, Switzerland: catalytic architecture
  in, xiii; Kramgasse in, ix, x
Boston: Commonwealth Avenue, 126;
  Government Center, 46; Quincy Mar-
  ket, 118; Rossi and, 36, 41; streets in,
  126; transformed water tank in, 161
Boston Store, Milwaukee, 61, 69
Boulevards, in American cities, 138
Brewery, Milwaukee, 56, 156
Britain: design guidelines in, 168; func-
  tionalist plan in, 3; model towns in, 22;
  townscape school of, 5. *See also*
  London
Broadacres idea, Wright's, 20
Bronson Hospital, Kalamazoo, 78
Brooklyn, Esplanade, 143
Broome, Oringdulph, O'Toole, Rudolf
  and Associates, 118
Brown, Denise Scott, 129, 131
Browne, Kenneth, 5n, 6
Buildings: in American cities, 129–33; in-
  dustrial production of elements of, 10;
  loft, 130–32, 133; as monuments, 130,
  161; styling of, 94, 132–33; values and,
  44. *See also* Architecture; Historically
  significant buildings/neighborhoods
Burlington Arcade, London, 39

C & O Canal, Georgetown, 91, 93
Cadillac-Fairview scheme, Portland,
  96–99
Caen-Herouville, design for, 10

181

Designer: Sandy Drooker
Compositor: G&S Typesetters, Inc.
Text: 10/12 ITC Garamond Book
Display: Phototypositor Helvetica Black
Printer: Malloy Lithographing, Inc.
Binder: John H. Dekker & Sons